**VOLUME 1**  **2021**

# HAYMANOT JOURNAL

KATABI (editor): Vince L. Bantu
ASSOCIATE KATABI (editor): Jacqueline Dyer
SGH MAMHERS (advisory board): Tim Allison,
Vincent Bacote, Vince L Bantu, Quonekuia Day,
Jacqueline Dyer, Carolyn Palmer, Cleotha Robertson, Nicholas Rowe

GENERAL KATABI
## VINCE L. BANTU

ASSOCIATE KATABI
## JACQUELINE DYER

Copyright © 2021 by Vince Bantu and Jacqueline Dyer, Editors

All rights reserved.

No part of this book may be reproduced or transmitted in any form or by any means, electronic or mechanical, including photocopying, recording, video, or by any information or retrieval system, without prior written permission from the publisher except for the use of brief quotations in a book review.

Published in the United States by Urban Ministries, Inc.
P. O. Box 436987
Chicago, IL 60643
www.urbanministries.com

ISBN 978-1-68353-851-6 (paperback)
ISBN 978-1-68353-852-3 (ebook)

All scripture quotations, unless otherwise indicated, are taken from the King James Version (KJV) and the New International Version (NIV).

Printed in the United States of America

Please visit www.meachum.org

# Table of Contents

1. "An Introduction to the Society of Gospel Haymanot". . . . . . 1
   Vince L. Bantu

   *Dersat*
   Umfundi: Quonekuia Day

2. "Raising Our Voices: A Missional Reading of Acts 16:35-40". . 11
   Dennis R. Edwards

3. "Dr. Cain Hope Felder: Life, Ministry, and Thought" . . . . . .24
   Ernest D. Gray Jr.

   *Sankofa*
   Umfundi: Vince L. Bantu

4. "Evidence of Orthodox, Anti-Arian Christianity and Geopolitical Independence of the Fourth-Century Axumite Kingdom as Provided by Inscription DAE 4" . . . . . . . . . . . . . . . . .38
   Dwayne T. Brown

5. "From Good News to Fake News: Christian Nationalism, Evangelical Apostasy, and Lessons for the Black Church". . . .46
   Christopher Barnes

6. "Rit'at of Ag'azi: Patristic Visions of Black Orthodoxy" . . . . 63
   Vince L. Bantu

   *Haymanot*
   Umfundi: Vincent Bacote

7. "A Sankofa of the Trinity: African Patristics and Ancient Trinitarianism Informing the Praxis of the Black Church". . . . 83
   Brooke D. Giles

8. "Black Lives Matter: Inside the Womb and Out" . . . . . . . 105
   Aaron Turner

   *Ujamaa*
   Umfundi: Jacqueline Dyer

9. "Embodiment and Orality: Methodology Mined from African Diaspora Formed Preaching for the Homiletics Classroom". . 113
   Jaclyn P. Williams

10. "An Onramp to Economic Shalom: Lessons from the Book of Ruth" . . . . . . . . . . . . . . . . . . . . . . . . . . . 129
    Luke Brad Bobo

11. "Ujamaa: Sacred Work in a Whole New World" . . . . . . . 145
    Jacqueline Dyer

12. "The Principle of Subsidiarity and John M. Perkins' Model of Christian Community Development" . . . . . . . . . . . . . 157
    RaShan A. Frost

# Book Reviews

"Review of Willie James Jennings' *After Whiteness:
An Education in Belonging*" . . . . . . . . . . . . . . . . . . . 171
Vince L. Bantu

"Review of Lisa M. Bowens' *African American Readings of Paul:
Reception, Resistance, and Transformation*" . . . . . . . . . . . 175
Dennis R. Edwards

"Review of Esau McCaulley's *Reading While Black: African
American Biblical Interpretation as an Exercise in Hope*" . . . . 179
Cleotha Robertson

"Review of Eric C. Redmond's *Say It!: Celebrating Expository
Preaching in the African American Tradition*" . . . . . . . . . . 183
Jaclyn P. Williams

# An Introduction to the Society of Gospel Haymanot

Vince L. Bantu

What is Gospel Haymanot? "Gospel" is from the Greek *euangelion* meaning "good news." This word refers to the reconciliation between Tilli (Nub: "God") and humanity through the finished work of Yeshua the Messiah. "Gospel" has also been a definitive marker of the Black Christian experience with regard to the unique musical tradition that has developed in the Black Church in the U.S. The word *haymanot* is a word in various East African Semitic languages that has been used for millennia in reference to "faith," "doctrine," "belief" and "theology." Used together, the phrase Gospel Haymanot represents a theological framework from the perspective of African and African-descended Nazrawis (Eth: "Christians") that is centered on the Gospel of our Lord and Savior Jesus. Gospel Haymanot brings the resources of academic theology to further develop the lived Black churches that are dedicated to the universal truth of the Gospel and the liberation of Black People.

In his definitive work *Proclamation Theology*, New Testament scholar and Christian Methodist Episcopal Bishop Joseph A. Johnson, Jr. defines Black Christian Theology thusly:

> Black Christian theology is a systematic interpretation of the meaning and significance of the Christian Faith for the worshipping, witnessing, proclaiming Black Christian

community. It seeks to analyze the condition of the Black man in the light of God's revelation in Jesus Christ. Its purpose is one of creating a new understanding of the dignity of Black men and women as children of God. Black Christian Theology is Christian Theology precisely because it utilizes God's revelation in Jesus Christ as its points of departure and also as a norm for the interpretation of the meaning and significance of human existence. With this understanding of Blackness, several definitions of Black Christian Theology may be presented: Black Christian Theology is a theology of, by, and for black people which has come out of their experience in America. It is a way of looking at God, the life and teachings of Jesus Christ, self, and the world, in the light of the Black Experience.[1]

Johnson's work helped to provide one of the only alternatives to what has become the dominant voice in academic Black Theology since the emergence of the Liberation Theology perspective of James Cone. While both of these scholars published their first books within a year of one another, Cone's work has far eclipsed that of Johnson in terms of influence for contemporary Black Theology in academic contexts. However, the theology of Johnson more closely resembled that of the Black Church in the U.S. Not only because Johnson was a bishop in the C.M.E. Church (who also published his books), but Johnson also strongly embraced the universal truth of the Bisrat and the divine inspiration of the Shajeh (Coptic: "Word," i.e., "Bible").[2] The project of Gospel Haymanot differs from the paradigm of Johnson's Proclamation Theology in two important respects: 1.) Johnson's failure to represent Black Theology in a manner inclusive of Black

---

[1] Joseph A. Johnson, *Proclamation Theology* (Shreveport, LA: Fourth Episcopal District Press, 1977), 129-130.
[2] Johnson, *Proclamation Theology*, 150.

women and; 2.) Johnson's particular focus on Black Theology as it has developed in the United States. A Gospelist perspective is one that understands the need for Black women theologians to be at the center of any Black theological paradigm. Likewise, Gospel Haymanot embraces a Pan-African understanding of common cultural values and experience of Black people around the world. However, Johnson's seminal work reflects many of the core traits of Gospel Haymanot.

## Rit'at

The word rit'at is used across many East African Semitic languages in reference to concepts such as "orthodoxy," "righteousness," and "justice." This word is often used in conjunction with haymanot with reference to theological orthodoxy. Among East African Nazrawis of antiquity, as well as most Black church contexts today, the value of rightly dividing the Word that we might be able to test teachings of false spirits has been highly esteemed.[3] The fifteenth-century Ethiopian *neguś* ("king") Zär'ä Ya'qob (1434-1468 CE) was also one of Ethiopia's most prolific authors in the area of haymanot. Zär'ä Ya'qob describes his Ethiopian nation as a people deeply devoted to rit'at: "So we now say to y'all, O people of Ethiopia of the orthodox faith (*retu'nä haymanot*), do not promote the false teachers who say that the Father and the Son and the Holy Spirit are one person."[4] It is true that Black Nazrawis have always placed great emphasis on freedom and liberation. This is evidenced in the fact that the first Black Nazrawis in the history of the Urpeh (Coptic: "Church") were deeply drawn to the injustice that our Lord and Savior faced, as prophesied by Isaiah.[5] However, precision and truthfulness in matters of haymanot have also been important as a mug to Black folk since day one. Can't nobody

---

[3] 2 Tim. 2:15; 1 Jn. 4:1.
[4] Conti Rossini, Karolus. *Il libro della luce del negus Zar'a Yā'qob (Maṣḥafa Berhān) II* CSCO 261/262, Scriptores Aethiopici 51/52 (Louvain: Secrétariat du SCO, 1965), 134.
[5] Acts 8:34.

say that Black folk don't care about truth or that concepts such as "orthodoxy" and "heresy" are white, Western concepts.

As Johnson stated in the above excerpt, the revelation of Tilli in the person of Yeshua is the point of departure for the Gospelist. The revelation of Yeshua, His Spirit and His Word are a divine, universal work. Haymanot, or theology, on the other hand, is a human work and is, therefore, culturally specific. Gospel Haymanot is indeed theology that is centered in the Black experience in all of its beautiful cultures. However, the Black experience and Black liberation are not the point of departure for Gospel Haymanot; they are, rather, the means to the end goal: which is Yeshua glorified. In this regard, Gospel Haymanot differs from the majority of academic Black Theology in its liberationist and womanist iterations precisely because of their tendency to place the liberation of Black people as the beginning and end of theology.[6]

## Sankofa

Sankofa is an Akan concept meaning "go back and get it," often used in the sense of reclaiming something that has been lost, taken or forgotten. This concept is often symbolized with an Akan image of a bird turning back and a stylized heart. This second image may even be attested in African-American burial grounds in the United States.[7] Culture is a beautiful thing that reflects the eternal diversity of the Trinity. Tilli (Nubian: "God") intended at creation for humanity to fill the earth and to cultivate it, the Seuartu Ngiss (Nubian: "Holy Spirit") spoke through every language of humanity at Pentecost and the multitude in Harm (Nubian: "Heaven") were of every culture in the world.[8] The Hebrew Apostles communicated the Bisrat (Eth:

---

[6] James H. Cone, *Black Theology and Black Power*, 7th ed. (Maryknoll, NY: Orbis Books, 2005), xii; Delores Williams, *Sisters in the Wilderness: The Challenge of Womanist God-Talk*, 2nd Ed. (Maryknoll, NY: Orbis Books, 2013), 40-41.

[7] Helena Woodard, *Slave Sites on Display: Reflecting Slavery's Legacy through Contemporary "Flash" Moments* (Jackson, MS: University Press of Mississippi, 2019), 56.

[8] Gen. 1:28; Acts 2:1-11; Rev. 7:9.

"Gospel") to Greeks by using cultural concepts and religious literature that already existed in the Hellenistic world.[9] The Persian Magi were drawn to worship the Messiah by the very religious means of astrology by which they worshipped prior to knowing Yeshua as Lord.[10] Cultural distinction is not merely a temporary reality but an eternal reflection of the beautiful diversity of Tilli. Because of the reality of sin, all human cultures both reflect the glory of Tilli and maintain values that are contrary to the Kingdom of Tilli. Nazrawis in every culture must disciple their cultures. This is a three-step process of: 1.) enhancing the aspects of culture that are in line with the Shajeh (Coptic: "Bible"); 2.) transforming and re-directing aspects of culture that have strayed from Tilli and; 3.) reject and avoid aspects of culture that are purely wicked.

This is a missiological process that all cultures must engage in by the leading of the Seuartu Ngiss, the Shajeh, indigenous Nazrawi leaders and in partnership with Nazrawis of other cultures. This process of cultural sanctification is wonderfully expressed by the African concept of Sankofa. Indeed, a haymanot of Sankofa is one that is unique to the Black experience and faithful to the Bisrat. Black Nazrawis must continue to cultivate forms of haymanot that are unique to the Black culture and experience. This is a crucial component of Gospel Haymanot. Black theologians must resist the desire to frame our discourse about Tilli and His Shajeh according only to white, Western categories. This is rooted in an overall tendency among Black people on both sides of the Atlantic: that is, to measure our success by the degree to which we achieve white goals according to white standards. This is not a call to reject or avoid white culture or theology.

We must embrace the strengths of Nazrawis of all cultures. However, there is a strong need to "go back and get" the African cultural values of our ancestors and contemporaries that have been

---

[9] Jn. 1:1-4; Acts 17:16-34; 1 Cor. 15:33; Tit. 1:12.
[10] Mt. 2:1-2.

vastly underemphasized. If indeed "Black Lives Matter," then Black Haymanot Matters. Gospel Haymanot is primarily concerned with providing framing and conceptualization for haymanot that is decidedly Pan-African. Implicit in this value is yet another challenge for Black Nazrawis: we must define what it means to do haymanot in a uniquely Black way beyond our struggle for liberation and critique of white supremacy. So much literature on Black theology and religion has to do with injustice and combating racism. This is an important task, real talk. But what does it mean to be Black from a theological perspective, in addition to a struggle for justice? How does haymanot as expressed by Africans and African-descended people take unique form according to our cultural values? We all know that white supremacy, white privilege and white normativity exist and must be resisted. Gospel Haymanot takes as a given the call for justice. The biblical call for justice is expressed in the African concept of rit'at meaning, "right," "orthodox," and "just." This is similar to the biblical words *mishpat* (Hebrew) or *dikaiosune* (Greek) which encapsulate the values of individual righteousness and social justice together. People who seek to exacerbate systems of privilege and oppression continue to overlook the clear biblical mandate for justice; but this mandate has always been clear in the Shajeh as well as among Black Nazrawis. We seek now to expand the conversation to further reflect on how we can come alongside the existing Black Urpeh and provide academic haymanot framing. This does not mean that justice work must cease or slow down. Rather, Gospel Haymanot invites us to "go back and get" a vision of haymanot that is biblical and uniquely Black.

## Nsibidi

Nsibidi is an ancient African system of writing, symbolism and thought that developed in the Cross River region of southwestern Nigeria no later than the fifth century CE. This system of learning has been used to transmit knowledge for centuries and is still used in societies among various Igbo, Efik and Ekoi people groups. Nsibidi typically are communicated in the form of symbols that are inscribed on a wide variety of surfaces, including textiles, woodwork, pottery and stones. Nsibidi symbols were used in political, judicial, religious and relational contexts and were taught to children as a core form of education. Nsibidi was used across a wide variety of cultures in the Cross River region of Nigeria and even flourished among Africans brought as slaves to the Caribbean and southern United States. The core of Nsibidi is the symbol full of meaning. The wide variety of meanings and interpretations assigned to the various Nsbidi symbols attests to the flexibility and nuance with which the symbols bear and are ascribed meaning. Nsibidi is one of several ancient writing systems from Africa and attests to the intellectual hustle of Black people. African approaches to knowledge and education, like Nsibidi, are often rigorous, nuanced, and connected to all areas of human life. Indeed, the word Nsibidi is often thought to refer to the concept of letters; that is, the communal process of studying and forming symbols that have changing and nuanced meaning that correspond to various aspects of the world.[11] Nsibidi is more than an ancient writing system from Nigeria—it is emblematic of rigorous Black approaches to the transmission of knowledge.

The value of Nsibidi—rigorous dedication to literature and its interpretation—has been a core value of Black people from jump street. The first recorded Black Nazrawi in history—the Kushite eunuch in Acts 8—was a learned scholar who had no trouble reading the scroll of Isaiah in Hebrew.[12] One of the first seminaries was in Egypt, also the site of the earliest biblical fragment. Many of the most prolific Nazrawi authors came from Africa, such as Tertullian, Cyprian, Origen, Augustine, Athanasius, Cyril, Pachomius, Shenoute, Severus ibn al-Muqaffa, Giyorgis of Sagla, Krestos Samra, Zar'a

---

[11] Molefi Kete Asante, *The Afrocentric Idea* (Philadelphia, PA: Temple University Press, 1998), 72.
[12] Acts 8:30-35.

Ya'qob and Walatta Petros. Real talk, just the simple fact that the earliest, well-known Black figures in the U.S. and Europe—such as Phyllis Wheatley, Frederick Douglass, Jupiter Hammon, Olaudah Equiano, Ignatius Sancho and Ottobah Cugoano—were learned scholars demonstrates the degree to which scholarship has been at the core of Black people from day one. After being stolen from his native West Africa, living as a slave in the Caribbean and Europe, being emancipated, becoming a Nazrawi and joining the abolitionist movement in England, Ottobah Cuguano said this regarding the value of his education and spiritual conversion:

> Thanks be to God for his good providence towards me: I have both obtained liberty, and acquired the great advantages of some little learning, in being able to read and write, and, that is still infinitely of greater advantage, I trust, to know something of Him "who is that God whose providence rules over all…How wonderful is the divine goodness displayed in those invaluable books the Old and New Testaments, that inestimable compilation of books, the Bible? And, O what a treasure to have, and one of the greatest advantages to be able to read therein, and a divine blessing to understand![13]

Cuguano utilized the education that was given to him to fight against the very evil that brought him to Europe in the first place. He dedicated himself to the studying of Scripture in order to provide a thorough exegesis of the Shajeh to argue against the idea that Black people are cursed and destined for slavery—the reigning view in the white world of the nineteenth century. The namesakes of the Meachum School of Haymanot are the abolitionists, pastors and scholars John and Mary Meachum. John and Mary founded the first Black church west

---

[13] Ottobah Cugoano, *Thoughts and Sentiments on the Evil and Wicked Traffic of the Slavery and Commerce of the Human Species* (Cambridge: Cambridge University Press, 2013), 13-14.

of the Mississippi in 1817 in St. Louis, MO. The Meachums pastored current and runaway slaves in the First African Church where they also employed them in a carpentry shop and educated them in the church's seminary. When Missouri laws prohibiting Blacks to read closed the school down in St. Louis, the Meachums moved their school onto a boat on the Mississippi River, away from Missouri jurisdiction. It was on this same river that Mary Meachum was later arrested for helping slaves escape Missouri into freedom.[14]

There is a rich and vibrant Black Urpeh tradition that is equally committed to the universal truth of the Bisrat and to social justice. However, this wholistic Gospel Haymanot has not largely been reflected in academic theology. Indeed, the overwhelming majority of Black scholars of religion and theology have departed from the haymanot of the Black Urpeh and have embraced an expression of white, mainline, liberal Christianity. This is the perspective that all of the accredited, Black seminaries in the U.S. teach from as well as the few existing Black academic conferences and journals. Indeed, academic Black theology has been hijacked by white, liberal theology. It is disingenuous to call this "Black Theology" as this theology does not reflect the haymanot of the Black Urpeh. Most Black Nazrawis believe that Yeshua is Lord and Savior and the only path to salvation and that the Shajeh is His divinely inspired, perfect Word. The overwhelming majority of Black seminaries and scholars do not. There is a major disconnect between the Black Urpeh and the Black Academy. The Society of Gospel Haymanot exists to be used by Tilli to rectify this janky situation. For this reason, this society holds the ancient African practice of Nsibidi—rigorous learnedness—as a core value. There are many Bible institutes and popular conferences in the Black community, and this is a very good thing. This Society exists to complement the Gospel ministry in the Black Urpeh and community

---

[14] John A. Wright, *Discovering African American St. Louis: A Guide to Historic Sites, 2nd Ed.* (St. Louis, MO: Missouri Historical Society Press, 2002), 9.

by providing resources and framing in academic haymanot that is centered on the Lordship of Yeshua, expressed in uniquely Black ways.

The Society of Gospel Haymanot is a consortium of Black scholars of biblical and theological studies that is characterized by these three core African values: Rit'at, Sankofa and Nsibidi. As a society rooted in biblical orthodoxy, our primary purpose is the glorification of Yeshua and the proclamation of the Bisrat. Toward that end we seek to come alongside the Black Urpeh that raised us and provide theological research that draws humanity to Yeshua and celebrates Black culture.

# Raising Our Voices: A Missional Reading of Acts 16:35-40

Dennis R. Edwards

## Introduction

In Acts 16:35-40, the apostle Paul responds to Philippian magistrates after the remarkable night he and his co-evangelist, Silas, had in prison. Most popular treatments of the Philippian prison event focus on the conversion of the jailer while the apostle's response to those who would permit him and Silas to "go in peace" is overlooked. However, we find in the apostle's agitated response lessons regarding public protest, especially in relation to the criminal justice system. My examination of Acts 16:35-40 employs an African-American hermeneutic, which I relate to the practice of missional hermeneutics.

African-American hermeneutics is not monolithic. Perhaps no hermeneutical approach is. Even so, there are some shared assumptions among African-American interpreters, one of which may be the affirmation of God's identity as Liberator.[15] This is a core tenet of the Gospel Haymanot or Gospelist paradigm that undergirds this very journal. Salvation, in a full sense of the term, includes God's work to liberate humanity—spiritually and physically—from

---

[15] E.g., Bruce Fields, *Introducing Black Theology: Three Crucial Questions for the Evangelical Church* (Grand Rapids, MI: Baker Academic, 2001), 15

the clutches of sin and Satan.[16] The *missio Dei*, God's mission, is deliverance. For example, "Since, therefore, the children share flesh and blood, he himself likewise shared the same things, so that through death he might destroy the one who has the power of death, that is, the devil, and free those who all their lives were held in slavery by the fear of death."[17]

African-American hermeneutics is missional in that interpreters affirm God's rescue mission in the world. That liberating work is performed by God for, within, and by God's people. African-American (or Gospelist) biblical interpretation has historically rejected readings of the Bible that reinforce the systemic oppression caused by whiteness.[18] *Whiteness* refers not primarily to skin color, but to a perspective that determines access to power and privilege.

Missional hermeneutics is an interpretive strategy that focuses on the *missio Dei*, including how humans participate in that mission. This paper explores some of the ways that missional hermeneutics and African-American biblical interpretation overlap by looking at a text that frequently gets overlooked or minimized. Acts 16:35-40 is the epilogue to the evangelization of Philippi by Paul and Silas. Typically, contemporary retellings, especially in sermons, end with the conversion of the prison warden and not Paul's plea to the magistrates.[19]

What follows is:

---

[16] See J. Richard Middleton and Michael J. Gorman, "Salvation," in *New Interpreter's Dictionary of the Bible* vol. 5, ed. Katharine Doob Sakenfeld (Nashville, TN: Abingdon, 2009), 45-61.

[17] Heb. 2:14-15.

[18] See Emerson B. Powery and Rodney Sadler, *The Genesis of Liberation: Biblical interpretation in the Antebellum Narratives of the Enslaved* (Louisville, KY: Westminster John Knox, 2016) 83-95.

[19] E.g., William D. Shiell, *Acts: Preaching the Word* (Macon, GA: Smyth & Helwys, 2017), 127-32. This commentary, geared toward preaching, must of necessity be selective but serves as an example of how popular preaching on Acts 16 focuses on the conversion story but not Paul's agitation with the Philippian magistrates.

1. A brief discussion of missional hermeneutics and its relationship to African-American biblical interpretation.
2. An analysis of Acts 16:35-40.
3. Missional implications of the passage from an African-American perspective.

A missional (Gospelist) reading of Acts 16:35-40 serves as biblical justification for the prophetic role that African-Americans often play in speaking the truth of police brutality and mass incarceration to the powerful of American society, which oftentimes includes professing Christians and not merely secular legal authorities.

## Missional Hermeneutics and African-American Biblical Interpretation

In recognizing the limitations of historical criticism for the exegesis of Scripture, various interpretative strategies have emerged that fit within the broad category of postmodern biblical interpretation.[20] One such approach is *missional hermeneutics*, defined as "an interpretive approach that emphasizes engaging Scripture to discern and participate in the *missio Dei*."[21] George R. Hunsberger offers a more robust definition and analysis of missional hermeneutics in his essay, "Proposals for a Missional Hermeneutic: Mapping the Conversation."[22] Missional Hermeneutics has four streams of emphasis, according to Hunsberger:

---

[20] Dennis R. Edwards, "Hermeneutics and Exegesis," in *The State of New Testament Studies: A Survey of Recent Research*, ed. Scot McKnight and Nijay Gupta (Grand Rapids, MI: Baker, 2019), 63-82.
[21] "Glossary" in *Scripture and Its Interpretation: A Global, Ecumenical Introduction to the Bible*, ed. by Michael J. Gorman (Grand Rapids, MI: Baker Academic, 2017), 416.
[22] The essay, delivered at the 2009 Society of Biblical Literature/American Academy of Religion gathering, can be found online: https://gocn.org/library/proposals-for-a-missional-hermeneutic-mapping-the-conversation/

1. The missional direction of the biblical story.

   God is on a mission. The Father sends the Son (John 3:16) and the Son sends his disciples (Matt 28:19; John 20:21). Missional hermeneutics discerns a metanarrative of Scripture and that overarching story describes a God on the move.

2. The missional purpose of the writings.

   Hunsberger recognizes a "missional theology" in the biblical writings, by which he means that the Scriptures serve to equip God's people to join God in mission. Part of what the Bible does is disclose our basic identity as humans who are called to do God's will and also to help us discern how to carry out God's will.

3. The missional locatedness of the readers.

   Missional hermeneutics not only considers the God-toward-humans perspective (i.e., God as actor in mission and communicator in Scripture), it also considers the humans-toward-God perspective. This is to say that who we are and where we are in the world is a factor in interpreting biblical texts. Who we are and where we are—our social location—had been disregarded in white/Western/dominant culture's historical-critical interpretation, as if there exists an objective and conclusive understanding of every Scripture passage. The Gospelist perspective understands that the lenses we bring to biblical texts color our interpretations and conclusions.

4. The missional engagement with cultures.

   The NT demonstrates how early Christians applied the teachings of the OT to their cultural situations in light of their experience with Christ. In a similar way, all followers of Christ throughout time have applied the teachings of the Scriptures in light of their experience with Christ to address a culture significantly different than that of the first readers of the Bible.

By employing Hunsberger's taxonomy, it becomes evident that African-American biblical interpretation employs a missional hermeneutic. First, African-American biblical interpretation recognizes the *missio Dei*, the mission of God, as fundamentally a rescue operation. God is a liberator. The book of Exodus has long served as the quintessential picture of God as deliverer, as Vince Bantu notes in *Gospel Haymanot*.[23] As James H. Evans, Jr. asserts, "the content of God's *revelation* is *liberation*."[24] Likewise, in the NT, Jesus exclaims: "For the Son of Man came not to be served but to serve, and to give his life a ransom for many" (Mk. 10:45). The language of ransom, to people enmeshed in a world where slavery was commonplace, evokes emancipation—freedom from captivity.

Second, African-American biblical interpretation serves to connect the liberating work of God to our own efforts to free those in captivity—spiritually as well as materially. A missional component of African-American biblical interpretation is its invitation to question oppressive readings of Scripture. Such interpretive efforts coincide with other postmodern approaches to biblical texts, especially Liberation Theology and Womanist Interpretation in resisting racist and otherwise oppressive interpretations of Scripture while advancing a "hermeneutic of wholeness."[25] Promoting the wholeness of African-Americans and women does not diminish the wholeness of others.

The third way that African-American biblical interpretation is missional is the obvious respect it gives to African-American readers, demanding we see ourselves as focal points within the biblical text and not ancillary to it. One simple example is the way many in the

---

[23] Vince L. Bantu, *Gospel Haymanot: A Constructive Theology and Critical Reflection on African and Diasporic Christianity* (Chicago, IL: Urban Ministries Inc., 2020), 7-8.

[24] James H. Evans, Jr., *We Have Been Believers: An African American Systematic Theology*, second edition (Minneapolis: Fortress, 2012, 10 (emphasis original).

[25] Raquel St. Clair, "Womanist Biblical Interpretation," in *True to Our Native Land: An African American New Testament Commentary*, ed. Brian Blount, et. al. (Minneapolis, MN: Fortress, 2007), 59.

USA have been conditioned to visualize most biblical characters as white, except for occasional individuals viewed as "ethnic," such as Simon of Cyrene who carried Christ's cross, or the Ethiopian official (who is not often pictured as in important African official, but as a lowly eunuch lackey. Even the Candace of Ethiopia—an important woman leader that Luke bothers to mention, is glossed over in retellings of the Acts 8 encounter with Phillip the evangelist). When African-American eyes are free to peruse the text, we see ourselves more clearly and engage the text with questions and commentary that white readers often miss.

Finally, African-American biblical interpretation engages our cultural practices. When recognizing that the Bible centers marginalized people, including the story of a Savior who was a marginalized Jew, African-American readers find resonance with our status and unique cultural practices. We learn to follow the early church's lead in applying Scripture to present situations under the guidance of the Holy Spirit, even with the obvious differences between the first and twenty-first centuries.

While much more could be said about the missional—i.e., Gospelist— nature of African-American hermeneutics, the issue at the moment is to consider how a frequently overlooked passage of Scripture speaks to the situation of many black people in the USA. The story of Paul and Silas in prison (Acts 16:16-40) is well-known to many churchgoing people, but the emphasis is typically placed on the conversion of the jailer and not what happens afterwards. Yet, the words of the agitated Apostle Paul in Acts 16:37, along with the response of the magistrates, affirms the godly mission of African-Americans particularly with regard to police brutality and mass incarceration.

## Philippian Hospitality

Philippi was a "first" (Luke uses *protos*) or "leading" city within Macedonia and a colony of Rome (Acts 16:12). The imperial backdrop is important, but beyond the scope of this paper. It is sufficient to acknowledge, however, that Philippians understood how power operated within the Roman Empire. Upon arriving in Philippi, Paul and Silas find Lydia down by the riverside and as this businesswoman receives the apostolic message, she gets baptized, along with her household, and offers the apostles hospitality, inviting them to stay in her home. Paul and Silas, however, briefly lose the comfort of Lydia's home and find themselves overnight guests of a Philippian jailer.

After going to pray (16:16), Paul and Silas get attacked by a frustrated mob that included businessmen who had lost a source of income when Paul exorcized a demon from an enslaved girl (16:16-22). The apostles are stripped, flogged, and imprisoned (16:22-24). Around midnight, however, while the apostles were praying and singing hymns to God while other prisoners paid attention, a violent earthquake strikes with enough power to unhinge doors and unloose shackles (16:25-27). The *desmophylax* (keeper of the prison, or warden), distressed over the possibility that prisoners had escaped under his watch, draws his sword in order to commit suicide. The warden's actions may be extreme to us, but Roman magistrates, to whom the warden was accountable, wielded significant clout. Christopher J. Fuhrmann stresses that "magistrates were doubly powerful, first by virtue of their office but also because they were by definition members of the local elite, whose importance to imperial society is hard to exaggerate…It was obviously dangerous to run afoul of a town's magistrates, especially when one's status was low."[26] Paul and Silas get the privilege of guiding the warden to become a follower of Jesus Christ, and as with Lydia, that jailer gets baptized along with his household. Paul and Silas receive hospitality once again from a new convert, as the prison warden feeds the apostles and nurses their wounds (16:34). This climactic episode is often the point where many preachers and teachers conclude the story of Paul

---

[26] Christopher J. Fuhrmann, *Policing the Roman Empire: Soldiers, Administration, and Public Order* (New York, NY: Oxford University Press, 2012), 58-59.

and Silas in Philippi. Yet, the interaction Paul has with the warden the next morning is especially relevant for African-Americans who, being citizens of the USA, are often not given the respect that white citizens are given when engaged by law enforcement.

## After Midnight in a Philippian Jail

In the morning, the magistrates send the *rhabdouchoi*, literally "rod-bearers" (Latin: *licotes*) (16:35), the "police" who beat Paul and Silas the previous day (16:22). The rod-bearers bring orders to "release these men," which the warden interprets as good news, as he reports to Paul that he and Silas can "go in peace." Paul, however, is agitated by the warden's report. Rather than leaving straightway, Paul protests. He accuses the magistrates of beating Silas and him in public without having been convicted in a trial. The magistrates are afraid (16:38) because the Roman *Lex Porcia de provocatione* "forbade under severe penalty the flogging of a Roman citizen."[27] According to Kavin Rowe, the aforementioned *Lex Porcia* was strengthened under Augustus by the *lex Iulia de vi publica* by preventing Roman citizens from being beaten, bound with chains, or having a yoke put around the neck.[28] Fuhrmann recounts an incident of a military policeman within the Roman Empire who was castigated by the governor for torturing a man without the presence of witnesses.[29] While the Romans were certainly not opposed to torture (after all, they perfected the horrible practice of crucifixion, for example), citizenship in the empire offered privileges.

Paul's protest resonates with African-American experiences and should get as much consideration as the conversion narrative that

---

[27] Joseph A. Fitzmyer, *The Acts of the Apostles: A New Translation with Introduction and Commentary*, AB 31 (New York, NY: Doubleday, 1998), 589.
[28] C. Kavin Rowe, *World Upside Down: Reading Acts in the Graeco-Roman Age* (New York, NY: Oxford University Press, 2009), 67.
[29] Fuhrmann, *Policing the Roman Empire*, 87.

precedes. Yet, as noted, there is a tendency to overlook this epilogue to the narrative. There are at least two ways that a white-centered reading of Acts 16 misses what an African-American reading catches. First, the emphasis on the conversion of the jailer bolsters the idea often touted that we should "just preach the gospel," and not be concerned about issues of justice. This perspective is part of the truncated way that white evangelicals tend to read the Scriptures. While the jailer's conversion is important—even critical—so is the prison context as well as Paul's challenge to the magistrates.

Second, within white evangelical circles, it is not uncommon to hear the assertion that Christians should not advocate for their "rights" because the only rights we have come from the Lord and not the State. Such an assertion serves as an attempt to silence the voices of the marginalized who hunger and thirst for justice. During the Civil Rights Movement, for example, white Christians—as well as some cautious African-Americans—questioned and challenged the appropriateness of public protests. Even today, BLM activists and many others who gather publicly to denounce police brutality are seen as a threat to the common good. Apparently, the police of today function similarly to the "rod-bearers" of the Roman Empire, using physical—and even lethal—force on people who appear to have little social capital.[30] I say "appear" because racial profiling has been a factor causing black and brown bodies to bear disproportional abuse by police. The system often appears impotent to deliver justice. African-American biblical interpretation draws us to Paul's assertion of his rights.

A Gospelist reading of Acts 16:35-40 provides biblical direction for public protests. Paul's complaint to the magistrates and demand that they personally visit the prison to engage the apostles in person shifts the power dynamic. Paul and Silas no longer appear as hapless

---

[30] See Esau McCaulley, *Reading While Black: African American Biblical Interpretation as an Exercise in Hope* (Downers Grove, IL: IVP Academic, 2020), 25-46.

and helpless victims, but as enlightened citizens, aware of their rights. This serves to "put the magistrates on the defensive."[31]

## Gospelist Implications of Paul's Response

I return to Hunsberger's categories of missional hermeneutics to point out some of the implications of an African-American Gospelist reading of Acts 16:35-40.

1. The missional direction of the story.

    Luke, the author of Acts, is the same author who recounts the Lord Jesus Christ's presentation of his own mission in Luke 4:18-19

    "The Spirit of the Lord is upon me,

    > because he has anointed me

    >> to bring good news to the poor.

    He has sent me to proclaim release to the captives

    > and recovery of sight to the blind,

    >> to let the oppressed go free,

    to proclaim the year of the Lord's favor."

    God's mission is to liberate us from oppression—spiritually and materially. After all, it was God who freed the captives in that Philippian prison, as the earthquake was certainly God's doing. Paul takes the opportunity to speak boldly to the magistrates, confident that God is the one who liberates. The apostles did not attempt to escape or seek retaliation in any way. They affirm that God is the liberator and also the one who validates our humanity even when the State fails to do so. Willie J. Jennings, in making clear that imprisonment and morality are not

---

[31] Joseph A. Fitzmyer, *The Acts of the Apostles: A New Translation with Introduction and Commentary*, AB 31 (New York, NY: Doubleday, 1998), 590.

necessarily connected, highlights the liberative work of God in this episode.

We have been brought into the space between people and prison systems through the Spirit who guides us into God's liberating work (Luke 4: 18-19). The disciples of Jesus cut through the quick and easy alignments of crime and punishment knowing that what constitutes a crime is a complex reality created at the intersection of public policies, government actions or inactions, and concealed private interests. Who gets arrested, charged, tried, and convicted is very often a matter of who has access to resources or who enters judicial processes already profoundly disadvantaged. This means that we resist the collapsing of our moral vision into the moral language that surrounds judicial systems and imprisonment. The question is not can a judicial or prison system be moral, but rather how must a disciple of Jesus give witness to its end and the beginning of a new way of life together?[32]

2. The missional purpose of the writing.

In a sense, Paul's plea for the magistrates to acknowledge their unjust treatment echoes the cries of Israel's prophets, such as Isaiah: "Is not this the fast that I choose: to loose the bonds of injustice, to undo the thongs of the yoke, to let the oppressed go free, and to break every yoke?" (Isa 58:6). Rebuking the authorities is often the work of prophets, who speak and act for God. The liberating work of God reverberates in the apostle's call for justice. Furthermore, Paul provides a lesson about peace and justice for the new converts, Lydia and the warden, and for all subsequent generations of Christians. God is committed to justice, which includes fair treatment of the vulnerable. The

---

[32] Willie James Jennings, *Acts* (Louisville, KY: Westminster John Knox, 2017), 168-69.

Roman Empire was certainly not US-type democracy, but the overarching message that God rebukes injustice is universal.

3. The missional locatedness of the readers.

    Our African-American lens on the text does not allow us to gloss over it but to linger with the notions of false imprisonment, police brutality, and the demand for justice. The story of Paul and Silas motivates us not to remain silent in the face of injustice, but to make our plea to the powerful to obey their own laws. Willard Swartley suggests that Paul and Silas sought an apology because peace seeks the restoration of relationships—even between citizens and the state—and is possible "only when misdeeds are duly acknowledged."[33] Although there is always the temptation to fight fire with fire, our faith compels us to live at peace with all people as much as possible (Rom 12:18). Within our history is the awareness that there can be no peace without justice ("no justice, no peace"). Yet we also know that retribution is not the way of Christ. Instead, we demand the acknowledgment of wrong—even on the part of the State. When evil is not acknowledged, hope dissipates, particularly for subsequent generations.

4. The missional engagement with culture.

    Paul's sense of justice was likely a product of his engagement with Israel's Scriptures. His Hellenistic background and status gave him confidence to bring his passion for justice to the secular Roman authorities. Kavin Rowe writes of a "reversal" motif in Acts 16:35-40, "With officials fearfully kowtowing before a pair of stubborn missionaries, the reversal in Philippi alerts the reader to the social and legal power of Paul's Roman

---

[33] Willard M. Swartley, *Covenant of Peace: The Missing Peace in New Testament Theology and Ethics* (Grand Rapids, MI: Eerdmans, 2006), 168–69. See also my discussion of this incident in *Might from the Margins: The Gospel's Power to Turn the Tables on Injustice* (Harrisburg, PA: Herald Press, 2020), 100-103.

citizenship and its significance for any conflict he might have with the state."[34] Paul's conflicts with the state did not arise because he was immoral or a lawbreaker. He was a victim of injustice. African-Americans can read the narrative of Acts 16:35-40 and see that when we are victims of injustice, one course of action that God sanctions is our calling secular authorities to abide by their own laws, intervene positively in the situation, acknowledge the injustice, and do whatever justice demands.

## Conclusion

African-American Gospelist biblical interpretation coincides with what has been called missional hermeneutics. Our approaches to Scripture ought to affirm the mission of God in the world, the role of godly people to follow God in that mission, the social location of Bible-readers, and the way culture and Scripture engage each other. An African-American Gospelist reading of Acts 16:35-40 demonstrates that African-American demands for justice, especially regarding the mass incarceration and police brutality that disproportionately affect us, finds robust support in the Apostle Paul's demands to Philippian magistrates. Christians who protest against injustice have the Apostle Paul setting a precedent.

---

[34] Rowe, *World Upside Down*, 68.

# Dr. Cain Hope Felder: Life, Ministry, and Thought

Ernest D. Gray Jr.

## Introduction

Some biblical scholars are cultural artisans, who craft methods and scholarship to build bridges from one generation to the next. In the life of Dr. Cain Hope Felder, we find an artisan whose life served as a veritable bridge to scores of students within the discipline of biblical studies. These students, the majority of whom are of African descent, would mostly agree that "he was a creative and visionary church leader and educator."[35] Equally unique and gifted, he quietly influenced these individuals to interpret scripture in liberative ways, and sought to instill the same posture within the communities he impacted.[36] These introspections will serve to ascertain the manner that Felder's impact continues to loom large beyond his life and will hopefully provide

---

[35] The Rev. Fred A. Allen executive director of Strengthening the Black Church for the 21st Century cf. Jim Patterson, "Scholar Who Focused on Bible's Diversity Dies," accessed, June 30, 2021, https://www.umnews.org/en/news/scholar-who-focused-on-bibles-diversity-dies.

[36] Among those known by this author to have been taught by Felder were Dr. Mitzi Smith professor of NT at Columbia Seminary, Dr. Brian K. Blount, president of Union Presbyterian Seminary and Dr. Rodney Sadler.

some insights into the various ways that he has impacted a generation of scholars.[37]

Felder's impact remains indelible due to a fierce defense of and presence within the Civil Rights Era as well as a staunch commitment to underrepresented scholars within the academy. For these individuals, Felder sought to historically rectify the modern agenda of Continental European theologians. He also improved and diversified the ways in which theological education was administered. In this brief history of interpretation, my interest lies within the reconstruction of his impact and the ways in which biblical studies benefitted from his investment in the realities of race within the scriptures.

Felder, in over four decades of teaching and scholarship, helped academics and church practitioners to wrestle with the implications of race, class, and social status throughout his writings. His scholarship unabashedly sought to keep his target audience in mind.[38] These reasons and others provide a compelling case for a closer inspection of his approach to biblical studies.

## Biographical Sketch

Cain Hope Felder was born in Aiken, South Carolina, a small town across from Augusta, Georgia in 1943. He moved to a segregated section of Boston with his parents and was fortunate to attend the

---

[37] Dr. Cheryl Sanders once remarked: "He was our champion and chief advocate for African-American engagement in advanced theological and biblical studies," Jim Patterson, "Scholar Who Focused on Bible's Diversity Dies," accessed June 30, 2021, https://www.umnews.org/en/news/scholar-who-focused-on-bibles-diversity-dies.

[38] In his introduction to *Stony the Road,* Felder was keenly aware that "there has been a critical need for blacks in the biblical field to become acquainted with and thereby become resources for each other…African-American graduate students in the biblical field have been few due to economic and political conditions that have kept their ranks small…Second, African-Americans who do gain entrance to graduate programs in Biblical studies must do so in overwhelmingly white graduate programs…Third, those African-Americans with the Ph.D. or Th.D. in biblical studies have often had to work in diverse settings," Cain Hope Felder, *Stony the Road We Trod: African American Biblical Interpretation* (Minneapolis, MN: Fortress Press, 1991), 2.

Church of All Nations. This experience would mark his future ambitions as he encountered a number of seminarians who attended Ivy League seminaries. His mother had a sixth-grade education, yet with the aid of a community of parishioners, he was able to attend the Boston Latin School where his exposure to multiple languages would grow. By the time he attended Howard University as an undergraduate, Felder would have had extensive language exposure. While at Howard, Felder majored in philosophy and minored in Greek and Latin. He was dedicated to the study of language later in life, and even desired to learn Arabic. While matriculating at Howard, he would go on to spend a year at Mansfield College at the University of Oxford where he earned a diploma in theology and further extended his linguistic acumen by acquiring Hebrew. Yet even in a different country, the realities of racial segregation were acutely felt. At Oxford and around the time of Dr. Martin Luther King Jr's death, he led a march to commemorate the life of Dr. King. He lamented that "British people had more solidarity with US Blacks than the US."[39] This paradoxical reality emerges even as Britain has had an unquestionable history of imperial conquest. Concomitant to this time in England, in 1969 Felder was asked to write a book review of Dr. James Cone's *Black Theology and Black Power*. This task encouraged him to continue to advance his studies in theological education. The trajectory of his academic career would solidify as he enrolled in Columbia University in order to earn his Ph.D. His thesis "Wisdom, Law and Social Concern in the Book of James," was completed in 1982. Felder assumed an adjunct position at Princeton University where he taught New Testament language and literature. While at Princeton, many students appreciated his teaching and stance on social justice issues.

---

[39] Insight into Felder's journey is captured in the two part series of the National Black Church Initiative compiled by Anthony Evans, "Black Theological Forum- Dr. Cain Hope Felder part 1-2" YouTube video, 49:53, July 13, 2012,
https://www.youtube.com/watch?v=DIBTcrFXxLM.

## Careers and Intellectual Influences

Fresh out of Columbia, Felder went on to teach as an adjunct at Princeton and would influence scores of future academicians and church practitioners. Here, Felder sought to challenge the well-established contentions regarding an expansion upon ethnic diversity. Novel in his approach, Felder pressed the reality that as a Middle Eastern Jew, Jesus the Nazarene— while not black—would not have been considered Caucasian by today's standards.

Admittedly, Felder experienced the dichotomy of hope and expectation while traversing the sour realities of racism. While at Princeton (1978-1981), much of the work conducted within the Civil Rights Era influenced his Bible-based activism. As Rev. Gilbert H. Caldwell, the founder of Black Methodists for Church Renewal notes: "His boldness in writing and talking about race and racism and black presence in Scripture, filled the void caused by silence and denial of others."[40]

It is apparent from the years of service in the academy that Felder sought to leave a lasting impression. His presence alone made a statement to the guild of New Testament studies that interrogating white Western normativity will foster a better understanding of the Scriptures and the African influences contained therein. Behind his imprint on the two main universities where he taught, Princeton and Howard, many recall his scholarship as well as the personal investment he made upon each student. Among those whose lasting impression promoted them to follow in his footsteps were Dr. Brian K Blount and Dr. Mitzi Smith.

During his years at Howard School of Divinity, Dr. Felder deepened his resolve to increase Afrocentric readings and methods of interpretation. This expansion took shape in the areas of mentoring students, publishing, professional society work and ongoing dialogues between the church and the academy. For over forty years, his work

---

[40] Patterson, Jim. 2019. "Scholar Who Focused on Bible's Diversity Dies." Accessed, June 30, 2021. https://www.umnews.org/en/news/scholar-who-focused-on-bibles-diversity-dies.

showed that Scripture was full of racial diversity. As momentum grew, he mentored generations of scholars who agreed with his major assertion that race was being downplayed in scholarship. He also moved the professional societies to embrace his broadened vision to diversify theological pedagogy.

## Felder's Influencers

While his readings in the classics stand out as one of the most prominent features of Felders' program of interpretation, the import of two towering figures are redolent in his theological imagination. James Cone and Howard Thurman influenced Felder as he navigated an academy that would often misunderstand his aims and question his motives. In other words, as he occupied the realms of academia that were in the predominant custody of white males, he often encountered questions that many colleagues found perplexing.

For Felder, James Cone served as the doyen of Black hopes and aspirations. After he received the offer to review the 1969 text *Black Theology and Black Power,* Felder knew that Cone was able to emphasize black suffering in ways that white institutions would not. Instead, these institutions consistently ignored the plight of black suffering and economic deprivation. Felder wanted to join in this work of highlighting racial disparities, yet he wanted to communicate this reality from the margins. As a textualist, one who interpreted the religious language of texts, Felder's work would challenge the status quo of commentaries and readings by removing them from historic readings of privilege.

Whereas it was no surprise that Howard Thurman was influential for Felder, it did not escape his notice that Thurman was revered for his preaching. For Felder, Thurman was one of the original Christian mystics, as often noted. He agrees with Thurman regarding the preaching moment by concurring "the sermon is an act of worship in which the preacher exposes his spirit and mind as they seek to reveal the working of the spirit of the living God upon them. It is a searching moment."[41] Though Thurman and Felder were not contemporaries, Thurman's impact noticeably drove Felder to see the black church as having "the necessary leadership to help Blacks become a truly free people with the ability to respond to life with courage, discipline, and vision."[42] These indispensable traits are seen within the lasting impact Felder had within the black church.

## Major Works: African-American Study Bible

Whereas orthodoxy might seem to be a moving target for Dr. Felder, with the release of this study bible, he shows his commitment to the Scriptures. He purports the centrality of the Scriptures within the Black experience. Unique to this text is its expanded cartography. Normally, maps within Bibles tend to show the area surrounding Palestine with just a sliver of northwest Africa, Egypt, the Nile Valley and Ethiopia. Felder sought to expand the maps within this edition to include more of the continent and its contributions to the history of the Bible.

## Stony the Road We Trod

Within the discipline of hermeneutics, there exists no shortage of texts to promote the reframing of synchronic, diachronic and existential methods.[43] In other words no dearth of scholarship exists to promote these rather ubiquitous forms of interpretation. It is within this arena that Felder edited a volume of methodological approaches that prior to 1991 had not been attempted in a single volume. This text, full of African-American biblical scholars, provided much needed examples of approaches that incorporate the lived experiences of people of color and their interaction with sacred texts. Four sections and eleven chapters in

---

[41] Felder, *Troubling Biblical Waters: Race, Class, and Family* (Maryknoll, NY: Orbis Books, 1989), 91; cf. Howard Thurman, *The Growing Edge* (Richmond, IN: Friends United Press, 1956), ix-x.
[42] Thurman, *The Growing Edge,* ix-x
[43] Michael J. Gorman, *Elements of Biblical Exegesis: A Basic Guide for Students and Ministers* (Peabody, MA: Hendrickson Publishers, 2009), 235-239.

total dedicated to the decentering of Eurocentric readings of Scripture sought to ensure that race, gender, and class were adequately addressed within biblical literature. Regarding this reality, Felder notes:

> (W)e must reckon with certain methodological problems in attempting to examine racial motifs as contained in the Bible. Ancient authors of biblical texts did have a color consciousness (awareness of certain physiological differences), but this consciousness of color/race, as we shall show, was by no means a political or ideological basis for enslaving, oppressing, or in any way demeaning other peoples.[44]

Hence by identifying the tendency to render these factors inoperative or at worst irrelevant, Felder charted a course toward ensuring that these aspects were not left behind. The entire collection of essays continues to advance the goal of critically engaging the text to present its liberative aspects. To this day, the text remains a standard regarding the advocacy of the Other and liberation approaches to exegesis.

## Troubling Biblical Waters

This text best evinces his careful consideration of the biblical texts in keeping with his ultimate concern to advance the discipline. In other words, in *Troubling Biblical Waters,* Felder sought to say what he had spent a lifetime preparing for. Freed by his mentors to make this text speak in a "black voice," he toiled over the tone and balance of his interlocutors to ensure that it was an accurate representation of his voice as a black scholar. After significant revisions to ensure that a balance was struck between the New Testament scholars of the discipline and the scholarship that they promoted, Felder returned to

---

[44] Cain Hope Felder, *Race, Racism, and the Biblical Narratives* (Minneapolis, MN: Fortress Press, 2002), 127. Cf. Nicholas F. Gier, "The Color of Sin/The Color of Skin," in *Journal of Religious Thought* 46.1 (1989) 42-52.

this work to ensure that his voice was represented accurately. Note this statement in chapter six:

> Freedom always costs. But, when great religious and social value is to be derived, one should not mind trying to pay freedom's price! In a recent collection of essays dedicated to the memory of the Black American mystic theologian Howard Thurman, Luther E. Smith contributes a chapter entitled "Community: Partnership of Freedom and Responsibility." At one point, Smith asserts that freedom is "experienced, nurtured and preserved through responsible involvement in the community." In this case, the *cost* of freedom is being "response-able" to the needs and hurts of others in the community. The idea is quite congenial with Paul's thoughts in Galatians 5:14, 15: "For the whole law is fulfilled in one word, 'You shall love your neighbor as yourself.'"[45]

It is the work of love that ultimately earned Felder the ability to respond to the scholarship that was absent from his formal education knowing that in doing so he would incur the ire of his white counterparts. In sum, *Troubling Biblical Waters* provided space for Felder to recognize that "black people of the diaspora have contributed significantly to humanity and they've rarely been recognized." He adds: "We've been harassed, cajoled, characterized and time has passed to set the record straight."[46]

---

[45] Felder, *Troubling Biblical Waters,* 114. Emphasis original. What remains salient within this excerpt is its social concern, which plays prominent roles within the letters of Galatians and James, both of which are elaborated in great detail in chapters six and seven respectively.
[46] Anthony Evans, "Black Theological Forum- Dr. Cain Hope Felder part 1-2" YouTube video, 49:53, July 13, 2012 https://www.youtube.com/watch?v=DIBTcrFXxLM

## True to Our Native Land

This text was published in 2007. Felder's former student and colleague Brian K. Blount served as general editor with Felder, Clarice Martin and Emerson Powery serving as associate editors. As a compilation of theological reflection, the attempt in this volume was to embed the unique historical, social, cultural, religious, and political realities that have shaped African-Americans with their interaction with the Bible in general and the NT in particular. In other words, *True to our Native Land* continued the work that *Stony the Road* inaugurated. It contains introductory essays that frame the discussion and address the impact of slavery, iconography, Pauline interpretation, hermeneutics, Womanist interpretation, homiletics, and art. Subsequent chapters engage in classic exegetical exposition while imbued with insights that connect the reader to the cultural, social and historic plight of Black Indigenous people of color (BIPOC).

## In His Image

Finally, as a lesser-known book from Felder's catena of written scholarship, *In His Image* connected with the iconography of African images by combining the reflections of Felder with the artistry of Letterio Calapai. With an abundance of etchings and the inspiration of Felder, the reader is invited to gaze upon familiar stories in this text from a decidedly African perspective.

## Methodology: Black Theology in Dialogue

For Felder, as for many within the ethos of Africana, dialogue represents an aspect of the Black experience. It is the way exchanges between a congregation and preacher engage the biblical text. It is also redolent within the scholarship of Felder. Within the text *True to Our Native Land,* Felder expositing the book of 2 Thessalonians sought to employ text boxes which highlighted some aspects of African-American culture, history, and values that the biblical text could address. Note well the manner that election in 2 Thess. 2:13-17 is discussed in tandem with Lerone Bennett's, *Before the Mayflower*:

> (T)he author makes a most important declaration: "because the Lord chose you." The appeal to the idea of special "election" or "being chosen" has been a period theme in African American History. One example of this is found in the fiery rhetoric of the celebrated "Walker's Appeal" of September 28, 1829, published in Boston by the free born David Walker."[47]

Such concomitant readings not only serve to enhance the experiences for readers of color, they demonstrate the intuitive nature that such readers have historically approached sacred texts. For this purpose, the following observations remain introductory.

## An Emphasis Upon Pluralism

Cain's work informs a pluriformity of positions regarding the characters within the Scriptures. To annotate these features is an act of decentering. If Eurocentric readings sought to minimize the pluralism in the Bible, Felder tried to uphold them:

> I hope to clarify, for modern readers, the profound differences in racial attitudes between those in the biblical world and in the subsequent history of Eurocentric interpretation. In Antiquity, we do not have any elaborate definitions of or theories about *race*.[48]

Here lies the dilemma with such theories. Within instances of sacralization—"the transposing of an ideological concept into a

---

[47] Cain Hope Felder "2 Thessalonians," in *True to Our Native Land: An African American New Testament Commentary*, ed. Brian K. Blount (Minneapolis, MN: Fortress Press, 2007), 406.
[48] Felder, *Race, Racism*, 127.

tenet of religious faith (or a theological justification) in order to serve the vested interest of a particular ethnic/racial group"—Felder found instances of this phenomenon. Most notable remains the text surrounding the curse of Ham, Gen. 9:18-27. To be clear the process of sacralization was not, according to Felder, at fault in the instantiation of the texts. Felder notes: "It becomes problematic when the meaning of ancient texts assumes a normative character as canon centuries later."[49]

## Theological Openness

Ideological Criticism is an approach that tries to uncover the system of ideas and ideals within the history of interpretation, which serves as the umbrella from which Felder deployed his methodology.[50] As one who drew from the context of the oppression of others within the dominant political and social classes, Felder made strides to uncover black theology hidden in plain sight and constructive interpretation, which promoted the issues of justice more prominently.

## Constructive Interpretation

Several themes can be elucidated from the texts of Felder. He ameliorated the *status quaestionis* in addressing the abeyance of racial diversity in the Scripture. It is evident that within his writings Felder sought to provide a textual and linguistic analysis of the cultures of the Ancient Near East not from standard-bearers but from the underrepresented communities that were in existence at the time.

Felder's hermeneutic *in nuce* is liberative. His approach toward arcane texts is to ameliorate their production, reception and import

---

[49] Felder, *Race, Racism*, 128-129.
[50] It is worth noting that openness does stand as an interpretive virtue along with criticizability, humility and generosity. Therefore, for Felder to employ openness suggests a general sense of expectation toward less dogmatic and potentially wider readings of a Biblical text.

within the communities they emerged from. Hence, the outworking of such a schema employed an eclectic approach toward all texts noting their contribution and in full awareness that some readings of Scripture, within the realm of academic study of texts, might keep them in a veritable "sunken place." Such readings are prime candidates for the project that Felder sought to employ. His focus was singular: to ensure that tall hidden aspects of the text would come to light.

## Felder's New Testament Schematic

In order to annotate features of Felder's approach to New Testament texts, one must first acknowledge his incredible agency with language. From there he sought to make salient items in the biblical texts that addressed race, racialist tendencies, and secularization. As noted, from an early age, Felder acquired a love for languages that never diminished. He was equally comfortable examining texts in the Hebrew Bible as he was in the New Testament, and even sought to engage with Arabic to gain some familiarity with this language as well. With the acuity to engage texts coupled with a desire to address the relative colorblindness which pervaded majority world scholarship, Felder's desire was to ensure that the Black representation in the Bible was expressed and celebrated. This is what led him to publish two works that demonstrate the beauty of the African-American culture. The first, *The Original African Heritage Study Bible,* contained over a dozen essays elaborating upon the African presence in the Bible. This emphasis speaks to his overall commitment to ensure that the cultural heritage of people of African descent are given their proper exposure and that history rightly acknowledges their presence from biblical to current days.

Another recent text that accomplishes a similar goal was *In His Image.* Here, Felder partnered with Letterio Calapai, an Italian impressionist artist to offer readings of biblical characters from an

African-Centered Christian Perspective. By expanding his repertoire, we see that Felder's focus continues to be the full amelioration of African images, presence and promotion throughout biblical scholarship.

## Critiques

While conversations regarding the moving target of orthodoxy can be fruitful, it is a moot point within the appraisal of this scholar. Dr. Cain Hope Felder was proudly occupied with liberal theology and as such invited and welcomed pluriformity[51] within his scholarship. Later in life, he adopted a syncretistic perspective of the worldviews. In the assessment of his overall body of work, Felder has consistently lobbied for liberty in readings that challenge Eurocentric methodological approaches. For this reason, Felder's work was often criticized by biblical scholars whose commitments remain ostensibly tied to a narrow form of biblical interpretation. Criticisms of this sort are not only valid but likewise affirm the variety of theological commitments that are at work within a discipline such as biblical studies. Accordingly, it is necessary to comprehend the body of work that Felder has produced as a reaction to the overall approach of the Western Church, which involves more narrow forms of biblical interpretation such as the historical-grammatical approach. In light of this, Felder's works should be seen as nomadic with regard to his confessional commitments. At first glance though it might appear that he was committed to liberal dogma, when in fact he was perhaps more orthodox than many would concede.

---

[51] It is worth noting that Felder, given his penchant to include non-white and non-Western voices could be perceived as departing from the storied doctrinal teaching of continental European scholars. This must be held in tension, given the paucity of non-white and non-Western voices, a knee jerk reaction would be to label them all liberal. And this is exactly why this journal and society exist!

## Conclusion

The goal of this essay was to discuss the impact of Felder's life work on Bible scholars and theologians as well as to demonstrate the ways he organically updated existing biblical instruction. He accomplished this by emphasizing the experiences of people of color in the Bible. These acts are social justice actions at their highest.

As the title of this essay has indicated, this survey of Dr. Cain Hope Felder has paid tribute to a figure whose impact far exceeds his physical stature. Indeed, Dr. Felder was known for his consistent stance against racism and bigotry, yet his writings are what will live on for much longer, spreading the gospel truth in all of its brilliance and diversity. It is for this reason that in summoning the history of this scholar, the title doyen seems most apt. The field of New Testament exegetical theology has been saturated by white normativity. Felder broke into this arena given the relative scarcity of New Testament scholars in the American context. Therefore, this title not only applies to Felder in an appropriate way, but it also demonstrates his lasting impression upon the field.

# Evidence of Orthodox, Anti-Arian Christianity and Geopolitical Independence of the Fourth-Century Axumite Kingdom as Provided by Inscription DAE 4

Dwayne T. Brown

As one of the oldest, extant churches in history, the Ethiopian Orthodox Church provides a compelling apologetic—proving Trinitarian orthodox belief at the initiation of the Christian faith in Sub-Saharan Africa. DAE 4 in the Axumite stelae field stands as a vital testimony as it documents historical African-national autonomy and formulation of Christian belief. This is in contrast to the Roman Empire, which continued to oscillate between Trinitarian and Arian expression of the nature and personhood of God in the fourth century CE.

> Prior to the introduction of Christianity, evidence suggests that the inhabitants of modern-day Ethiopia and Eritrea were largely polytheistic—in close resemblance to the religion in ancient southern Arabia…The coinage inscriptions of pre-Christian Axumite kings containing the disc and crescent symbols, along with prominent stelae carvings of the sun disc and inscriptions to various gods indicate a pagan belief-system prior to the reign of the first Christian king, Ezana…In the pre-Christian

period the king was considered to be the son of Mahrem, who was identified with Ares, the Greek god of battles. He was probably the special dynastic or tribal god of the Aksumites. This relationship would have enhanced the kings' position in the eyes of his subjects, raising him to a quasi-divinity which set him in a special category, apart from and above all other men. The Aksumite royal inscriptions emphasize the king as a dynamic figure, son of a deity, member of one of the Aksumite clans…the leader of his people as war-hero and conqueror, but also as judge and lawgiver.[52]

## Pre-Christian Axumite Geopolitics

Axum was the capital of an African empire in modern-day northern Ethiopia and Eritrea that flourished throughout the first nine centuries of the common era. The early Axumite ruling philosophy or religious governmental system is consistent with the ancient systems in the Roman Empire throughout northern Africa, the Levant, western Asia and Arabia. The Axumite Empire is one of the first urban civilizations in Sub-Saharan Africa—strategically located for trade and communications between the Mediterranean countries and those bordering the Indian Ocean. Segments of the Axumite population were literate in Greek, which was the primary language of international trade with the Roman Empire during Late Antiquity. Nevertheless, the classical Ethiopic language, Ge'ez, remained the dominant spoken and written language of the Axumite Empire.

The Kingdom of Kush, to the north of the Axumite Empire, was a close and formidable rival. Kush had much older trading networks that controlled much of the interior region of Africa and supplied Egypt with goods via the Nile corridor. However, by the first century CE,

---

[52] Stuart Munro-Hay, *Aksum: An African Civilization of Late Antiquity*. (Edinburgh: University Press, 1991), 57, 124.

Axum gained control over territory previously Kushite. Approximately one hundred years prior to the reign of King Ezana, Axum began to control the western Tihama region of Southern Arabia, and during its ascension, began minting its own currency. Axum was also named by Mani, the Iranian prophet, as one of the four great powers of his time along with Persia, Rome, and China. At its height, Axum controlled northern Ethiopia, Eritrea, northern Sudan, Djibouti, Yemen, and southern Saudi Arabia (totaling 1.25 million km²).

## The Christianization of the Axumite Empire

The historian Tyrannius Rufinus details the conversion of King Ezana.[53] Socrates of Constantinople, a fourth-century Greek historian, provides a secondary account of the conversion in his *Ecclesiastical History*. Both accounts chronicle the narrative of Aedesius and Frumentius, two Syrian youths who were shipwrecked on the Ethiopian coast while traveling with a philosopher, Meropius, subsequently captured and brought to the royal court of Ezana's father. The two Syrians were Christians who gained the trust of the ruling queen and in servitude, eventually became royal cupbearer and imperial treasurer.[54] The boys became confidants of a young Ezana and when he became the King of the Axumite Empire, he freed the young men.[55] Frumentius became the first bishop of Axum and the primary evangelist leading the successful conversion of the young King Ezana to Christianity.

Following in the traditions of many empires and preceding rulers, King Ezana inscribed his successful military campaigns and conquests on public stone fixtures. Four extant inscriptions of Ezana document his victories and secondarily, his religious identity. The first two inscriptions,

---

[53] Stephanie L. Black, "In the Power of God Christ": Greek Inscriptional Evidence for the Anti-Arian Theology of Ethiopia's First Christian King," in *BSOAS* 71, 93-110 (2008): 96.

[54] Black, "In the Power of God Christ," 97.

[55] Philip R. Amidon, *The Church History of Rufinus of Aquileia: Book 10* (New York, NY: Oxford University Press, 1997), 18–20.

labeled Inscriptions 1 and 2 (DAE 4 and DAE 4, respectively), detail the conquering of a rebelling ethnic group. In these inscriptions, Ezana displays his polytheistic belief system by describing himself as the "son of the unconquered god Ares," (*Mhrm* in Ge'ez). In the third Ge'ez inscription, which describes the victory over the Noba people, Ezana refers to "the Lord of Heaven" and "the Lord of all." This inscription omits any reference to Ares (*Mhrm*) and implies monotheism but comes short of expressing Christian or Trinitarian views. Stephen Kaplan details the debate concerning the dating and extent of Ezana's conversion on the evidence provided in the third inscription:

> While some scholars, including Conti Rossini, Guidi, Sergew Hable Selassie, and Bairu Tafla accepted the fact that Ezana had become a Christian, others, noting the absence of specifically Christian formulae in the inscription, offered differing interpretations. The Russian Scholar Yuri Kobichtchanov argued for a vague monotheism similar to that found in some South Arabian inscriptions. A. Z. Aescoly suggested that Ezana had become a Jew. Ephraim Isaac wrote that both the phrase "the Lord of heaven" and the use of the cross on Ezana's later coins were in keeping with strong "Jewish-Christian" tendencies in Ethiopian Christianity.[56]

While the third inscription marks a distinct departure from previous polytheistic beliefs, Inscription 4 (DAE 11) explicitly invokes a Trinitarian Christian God. Stephanie Black provided the following translation of the inscription:

> By faith in God and by the power of the Father and Son and Holy Spirit, to the one who saved the kingdom for me by faith in his son Jesus Christ, to the one who helped me and who always helps me, I, Azanas, king of the Aksumites and

---

[56] Kaplan, Steven. "Ezana's Conversion Reconsidered," in *Journal of Religion in Africa* 13.2 (1982): 101-109.

Himyarites and of REEIDAN and the Sabaeans and of SILEĒL and of KHASŌ and the Bejas and of Tiamo, BISI ALĒNE, son of ELLE-AMIDA, a servant of Christ, give thanks to the Lord my God. And I am not able to tell the full measure of his favour, because my mouth and my mind are not able [to tell] all the gracious things which he has done for me: that he made me strong and powerful and he gave me a great name through his son in whom I believed, and he made me leader of all my kingdom because of faith in Christ, by his will and the power of Christ; because he himself led me, and in him I believe and he himself became my leader. I went out to make war on the NŌBA, because the MANGARTHŌ and KHASA and ATIADITAI and BAREŌTAI cried out against them, saying, "The NŌBA have made us suffer. Help us, because they oppressed us, killing us". And I rose up in the power of God Christ, in whom I believed, and he led me. And I went up from Aksum in the Aksumite month of MAGABITHE, on the eighth day, a Saturday, by faith in God, and I reached MAMBARIA and from that place I provisioned [my army].[57]

According to Inscription 4, King Ezana attributes the military victory over the Noba people (Nubians) with a clear enunciation of Trinitarian Christianity, thanking Jesus for helping liberate oppressed people groups, securing the victory and allowing him command of a vast kingdom. Ezana is careful to articulate "he himself led me," which indicates a departure from past polytheism and into distinct monotheistic thought. Foremost in the written declaration is the phrase: "And I rose up in the power of God Christ, in whom I believed, and he led me." This statement reflects Ezana's Christian thought, as taught by Trinitarian Syrian advisors, and unambiguously acknowledges the divinity of Jesus Christ.

---

[57] Black, "In the Power of God Christ," 102.

Though the Roman Emperor Constantine ended the wholesale persecution of Christians in the Roman Empire in 313 CE, the predominant theology of the Roman emperor at this time did not hold Christ to have a divine nature or personhood in the Godhead. This belief system, Arianism, was a nontrinitarian form of Christian teaching originating with the Alexandrian priest Arius, in the early fourth century. Arians maintained that Jesus Christ, the Son of God, was created by God the Father and therefore subordinate, not coeternal or consubstantial. Athanasius of Alexandria was the primary defender of Trinitarian Christianity in Egypt and he affirmed the divinity of Christ. This greatly influenced Frumentius and subsequently Ezana's convictions.

Constantine sponsored the Council of Nicaea in 325 CE which declared Trinitarian belief as the dominant faith of the Roman Empire. However, his son and successor, Constantius, who came to power twelve years later, was less accepting of Trinitarianism and appeared to prefer an Arian interpretation of the nature of Christ. The emperor, Constantius, sent a letter to King Ezana advising him that Frumentius' consecration as bishop by Athanasius was invalid and that Frumentius must return to Constantinople to be re-consecrated by the Arian bishop, George of Cappadocia.[58]

Prior to the introduction of Christianity, Roman emperors were seen as divine[59] and even after the Christian conversion, the religious authority of the emperors was still absolute. Ezana had two options: capitulate to the Roman authority or remain resolute in his own principles and risk an antagonistic relationship with Rome. There is no evidence of Frumentius returning to be re-consecrated and therefore it can be reasonably concluded that he did not. This supports the idea that the Axumite Empire remained affirming the divinity of Jesus

---

[58] Kaplan, "Ezana's Conversion Reconsidered," 102.
[59] Andrew Erskine, *A Companion to the Hellenistic World* (Malden, MA: John Wiley & Sons, 2009), 443.

Christ, and established a Trinitarian Christian nation independent of a Romano-centric religious influence.

Contrasting the introduction of Christianity between the Roman Empire and the Axumite Empire, the differences cannot be more distinct:

> There was a fundamental difference between the way in which Christianity was introduced in Ethiopia and the way in which it was first introduced in the Graeco-Roman world. There, Christianity began among the lower classes and gradually after three centuries succeeded in gaining converts among some members of the royal family. In Ethiopia it was the other way around.[60]

## The Christian Axumite Empire and Its Contemporary Church Application

Axum's ascent and decline occurred in the span of approximately 1,000 years. Within that time, the Axumite empire was described as a formidable superpower that began to decline as a result of geopolitical and climate changes. Rare soil degradation, evidence of periodic flooding, erratic annual crop-irrigation and occasional pillaging by bordering tribes contributed to a relatively rapid decline of the empire.

King Ezana is the catalyst for the establishment of a regional superpower opposing imperial powers of his day and forming orthodox, Trinitarian Christianity in the Horn of Africa. This kingdom became the longest uninterrupted national Christian church body on the African continent and second only to Armenia within the history of Christianity. The nation did not adopt the culture, language, milieu of Hellenistic Rome in order to remain in existence. Axum produced Christian literature, decrees and culture within its own language and understanding, faithful to the Scriptures.

---

[60] Kaplan, "Ezana's Conversion Reconsidered," 104.

The Christian Axumite Empire should serve as the archetypical historical example for the African and African-American Christian church. Though Mussolini's Italian forces invaded and briefly occupied Ethiopia in 1935, then-emperor Haile Selassie regained control in 1941. Therefore, Ethiopia was one of the only nations (and only African nation) to have never been fully colonized by an external imperial government.

In this time of increased religious and political debate on the conditions of the African and African-American Christian church, its origins, alliances, influences and direction, it would be advantageous to reconsider the example of ancient Axum as a source of authentic cultural and spiritual pride, exemplifying steadfast conviction, anti-colonial history with anti-imperialist resistance.

This generation faces pressure to abandon their Christian convictions due to the popular and inaccurate assertion that all descendants of the victims of the Trans-Atlantic Slave Trade obtained their faith in Christianity through the force of their oppressors. The historical fact of the conversion of the Axumite Empire—over one thousand years prior to the Trans-Atlantic Slave Trade—contradicts the idea that the Sub-Saharan African did not accept Christ of their own free choice. Furthermore, even the documented narratives of the enslaved overwhelmingly show that force was rarely a factor in the acceptance of Christianity.[61]

In conclusion, the historical record of the Axumite Empire details an acceptance of orthodox Christianity, resistance to Roman influence, adherence to its own culture while expressing faith in Jesus Christ, survival of crippling decline and monumental resistance to oppressive imperialism. This period should be an indispensable subject taught in church history as an example of perseverance and God's Grace.

---

[61] Sally Ann H. Ferguson, "Christian Violence and the Slave Narrative," *American Literature* 68.2 (1996): 297-320.

# From Good News to Fake News: Christian Nationalism, Evangelical Apostasy, and Lessons for the Black Church

Christopher Barnes

## What Is Truth?

One of the hallmarks of the prophetic is to declare the timeless Truth of God through the changing generations. This is why Sankofa, "go back and get it," is essential. Without Sankofa, our attempts at the prophetic are, well, pathetic. And it is not meant as a cute comedic euphemism. One way "pathetic" can be defined is "pitifully inferior or inadequate."[62] Couple that with the word's Greek root of *pathos*, which in essence means "suffering," and what is the end result? An experience where everyone suffers from a pitifully inadequate prediction of where God is going due to the lack of a keen appreciation and understanding of where God has been.

Such is the case of the Jewish leaders during Jesus' crucifixion trials. As the scene begins in John's account, we see that they led Jesus from Caiaphas to Pilate.[63] However, upon approaching their

---

[62] *Merriam-Webster.com Dictionary*, s.v. "pathetic," accessed May 11, 2021, https://www.merriam-webster.com/dictionary/pathetic.

[63] Jn. 18:28-40. Unless otherwise indicated, all biblical references are taken from the New International Version (NIV).

destination, "so that they could eat the Passover, the Jewish leaders would not enter the palace; entering the palace would have made them ritually impure." If we read too fast, we miss the irony of the whole situation. The Jewish leaders were mindful enough to maintain ritual purity to partake in the Passover while being woefully and willfully ignorant of the impurities that caused them to kill the Passover lamb.

Because they did not fully appreciate and understand what God achieved in the first Passover, the Jewish leaders did not see what God was doing in their midst of their current one. Thus, in their lust for maintaining their perceived power, they settled for the performance of Passover over the point and power of it. And that act nullified their ability to be prophetic, to affirm and declare the Truth of their time.

It is then, no surprise that Pilate retorts to Jesus, "What is truth?" If the leaders of God's "chosen people" are off-kilter as to where God is, what hope is there for the rest of the world to discern Him? So the question is, while God indeed is within His right to hold Pilate responsible for his part in the crucifixion, given the contrasting representations of God presented before him, can Pilate be entirely blamed for his error?

And with what seems to be the American church's historical and current lust for power, as evidenced in the 81% white evangelical backing of President Trump in the 2016 U.S. election, is it any surprise, then, that the world struggles with the conceptualization and discernment of divine Truth?[64] How was this possible? How does one get from "good news"—the gospel—to "fake news?" How has the church arrived at this moment where she sacrificed the point and power of the gospel on the altar for the mere performance of it. That is, a mere perfunctory, tame, and hollow outward display of gospel living that

---

[64] Jessica Martínez and Gregory A. Smith, "How the faithful voted: A preliminary 2016 analysis," Pew Research Center, November 9, 2016, https://www.pewresearch.org/fact-tank/2016/11/09/how-the-faithful-voted-a- preliminary-2016-analysis/.

does nothing to challenge the current power structures, but gleefully jumps into bed with them?

Enter Christian Nationalism. This paper examines Christian Nationalism, its recent history, and its role in producing an 81% voter turnout for Donald Trump in 2016, and almost mirroring that number in November 2020. Some takeaways will then be offered for the Black church for the continuation of forming a Gospelist theology distinct from supremacist and nationalist ideology. In doing so, the Black church can avoid suffering a similar fate of irrelevance and destruction of witness within the culture it serves and maintain its prophetic voice.

## What Is Fake News?

It is appropriate to begin with understanding how the term has been used in recent discourse, how it is generally defined, and how I will use the term within this paper's context. While the term itself has existed since 1890, "fake news" has only recently re-entered public discourse in the last three years, with President Donald J. Trump. This began in January 2017 in the context of dismissing a reporter demanding a chance to question him on his ties to Russia. To be clear, as the term is traditionally understood and used, one can argue that in this case, and many other documented cases, his use of the term is grossly inaccurate and more so an exercise in irony.

There is no universally standard definition for fake news. For instance, David M.J. Lazer offers an often-cited definition:

> We define "fake news" to be fabricated information that mimics news media content in form but not in organizational process or intent. Fake-news outlets, in turn, lack the news media's editorial norms and processes for ensuring the accuracy and credibility of information. Fake news overlaps with other information disorders, such as misinformation (false or

misleading information) and disinformation (false information that is purposely spread to deceive people).[65]

However, Edson C. Tandoc examined several definitions to devise a typology for understanding the concept more holistically. His typology is based on two dimensions: 1.) facticity—how much of the fake news source is based in fact, and; 2.) intention—the intent of the author to mislead their audience. Various types of fake news are then able to be placed in a matrix, ranging from low intention, low facticity (i.e., mere news parody) to high intention, high facticity (i.e., native advertising). Tandoc then explores a factor in defining fake news that had not been previously—the audience: "While news is constructed by journalists, it seems that fake news is co-constructed by the audience, for its fakeness depends a lot on whether the audience perceives the fake as real."[66] In essence, it is within the mind of the audience that fake news derives its power.

So then, what makes a person susceptible to "fake news"? What makes "fake news" alluring to its audience? Joshua Tucker shared some preliminary findings from his ongoing research on Americans' ability to detect fake news. He noted that of 90 respondents tested, most were "pretty good at identifying true news," at a rate of about 70 percent. However, when it came to detecting "fake news," the detection rate was 30 percent. This calculation was regardless of age or education. The most important determining factor in the susceptibility to "fake news" was in the area of partisanship. Both liberals and conservatives were equally terrible at identifying fake news that aligned with their

---

[65] David M. J. Lazer, Matthew A. Baum, Yochai Benkler, Adam J. Berinsky, Kelly M. Greenhill, Filippo Menczer, Miriam J. Metzger, Brendan Nyhan, Gordon Pennycook, David Rothschild, Michael Schudson, Steven A. Sloman, Cass R. Sunstein, Emily A. Thorson, Duncan J. Watts, Jonathan L. Zittrain, "The Science of Fake News." *Science* 359, (2018): 1094–1096.

[66] Edson C. Tandoc Jr., Zheng Wei Lim and Richard Ling, "Defining 'Fake News': A typology of scholarly definitions," *Digital Journalism*, 6.2, 137-153 (2018), 148.

ideological beliefs.[67] In essence, the data showed that a person is more susceptible to be misled by "fake news" when it affirmed what they *wanted* to believe.

Of course, this is not surprising. Tucker's research findings confirm what Bible readers and scholars knew all along. At many points, the Bible has warned of humanity's capacity for deception as a result of misguided desires, beginning with the cause of humanity's Fall in the Garden of Eden. Of particular note for this study is Paul's warning to Timothy: "For the time is coming when people will not put up with sound doctrine, but having itching ears, they will accumulate for themselves teachers to *suit their own desires* (emphasis mine)."[68] Paul states how a community, a people, can digress from good news—the gospel—to "fake news." In the case of the church, "fake news" is a distortion of the truth of the gospel message to suit one's own selfish ends. And Christian nationalism has been the "fake news" of choice for millions of evangelicals, especially in 2016.

## A Brief History of Contemporary Christian Nationalism

It is understandable that 81% of white evangelicals voted for Trump and assume that evangelicalism has some severe problems. It is another thing to determine just what happened November 8, 2016. Whitehead and Perry argue that it was Christian Nationalism—not evangelicalism—that was more of a determining factor of how one voted in the 2016 presidential election. Whitehead and Perry outline four categories of orientations toward Christian nationalism they determined from their survey responses: 1.) Rejecters—outright opposing the idea of a Christian nation or Christian influence in

---

[67] Joshua Tucker, "The Truth About Fake News: Measuring Vulnerability to Fake News Online & Crowdsourcing Fact Checking," January 29, 2021, https://matrix.berkeley.edu/research-article/video-measuring-belief-fake-news-online/.
[68] 2 Tim. 4:3.

public policy in any way; 2.) Resisters—undecided but lean toward opposing Christian nationalism; 3.) Accommodators—undecided but lean toward accepting Christian nationalism and; 4.) Ambassadors—wholly supportive of Christian nationalism. Rejecters and Resisters are those who are unsupportive of Christian nationalism. Conversely, Accommodators and Ambassadors are supportive of the ideology.[69]

Each of these four orientations towards Christian nationalism has no bearing on racial identity, socio-economic background, or political affiliation. It is tempting to conclude that Christian nationalism is solely the product of "white evangelicals" based on the proliferation of Christian nationalist rhetoric among white, evangelical, and Republican Americans. However, this is an incomplete picture. In fact, 65% of African-Americans are more supportive of Christian nationalism (combining Accommodators and Ambassadors, with Accommodators making up 45%) than any other racial group. This is interesting to note, considering that African-American leaders such as Martin Luther King have employed certain Christian nationalist ideals and narratives in their appeal against racial oppression.[70]

The myth that the U.S. is a "Christian Nation" has always persisted in some form throughout U.S. history. Daniel K. Williams notes that "the nation has always been engaged in a struggle over its religious identity, with some members of the Christian majority always arguing with others over just how 'Christian' the nation should be."[71] In particular, the ideology of "Christian nationalism" in America has been historically linked with both political progressivism and conservatism. Given the fluidity of this ideology throughout American history, it is best to define the current iteration of "Christian Nationalism" that was heavily influential in the 2016 U.S. presidential election.

---

[69] Andrew L. Whitehead and Samuel L. Perry, *Taking America Back for God: Christian Nationalism in the United States* (New York, NY: Oxford University Press, 2020), 25-38.
[70] Whitehead and Perry, *Taking America Back for God*, 41; 225.
[71] Daniel K. Williams, "Baptizing Uncle Sam: Tracing the Origins of Christian Nationalism," in *Reviews in American History* 44.3, 391-399 (2016): 399.

Whitehead and Perry's definition has been helpful in understanding the current brand of Christian Nationalism. They define Christian Nationalism as:

> a cultural framework—a collection of myths, traditions, symbols, narratives, and value systems—that idealizes and advocates a fusion of Christianity with American civic life ... the "Christianity" of Christian nationalism represents something more than religion...it includes assumptions of nativism, white supremacy, patriarchy, and heteronormativity, along with divine sanction for authoritarian control and militarism. It is as ethnic and political as it is religious.[72]

People committed to "Christian nationalism," the idea that the United States is and has always been a "Christian nation," are more prone to an authoritarian leadership style, ethnocentrism, and racial prejudice.[73] Key conservative Christian leaders like Robert Jeffress lament over "the denial by secularists and even some professing Christians that America was founded as a Christian nation."[74] Jeffress defended President Trump's incendiary remarks concerning protections for immigrants from "s--hole countries," referring to Haiti, El Salvador, and African countries. Jeffress states: "Apart from the vocabulary attributed to him, President Trump is right on target in his sentiment."[75] Paula White-Cain, special spiritual advisor to President Trump, boldly asserted that opposition to the president is opposition to God.

---

[72] Whitehead and Perry, *Taking America Back for God*, 10.
[73] Whitehead and Perry, *Taking America Back for God*, 19.
[74] Robert Jeffress, *Twilight's Last Gleaming: How America's Last Days Can Be Your Best Days* (Brentwood, TN: Worthy Publishing, 2011), 4.
[75] Alex Samuels, "Texas Democrats react with outrage to Trump's "shithole" comment — with one calling for impeachment," *Texas Tribune*, January 12, 2018, https://www.texastribune.org/2018/01/12/what-texas-officials-are-saying-about-trumps-comment-shithole-countrie/

In her book, Katherine Stewart further explains how today's Christian nationalism has worked as a top-down movement and not merely a grassroots initiative. Its leaders, she states "have quite consciously reframed the Christian religion itself to suit their political objectives and then promoted this new reactionary religion as widely as possible, thus turning citizens into congregants and congregants into voters."[76]

Or as the late Rev. Jerry Falwell Sr., founder of Thomas Road Baptist Church and Liberty University, stated at the conception of the Moral Majority: "We have a three-fold primary responsibility: Number one, get people saved, number two, get them baptized, and number three, get them registered to vote."[77] Contemporary American Christian nationalism began to take shape when white Christian conservatives were motivated from a near half-century of political dormancy. Whereas most were not even registered to vote beforehand, many began to take a stand against, not abortion—which is the "fake news" commonly propagated in this case—but what they viewed as a federal government infringement on their right to operate tax-exempt segregated schools.

This new voting bloc, called the "New Religious Right," was the product of religious conservative political activist Paul Weyrich. Weyrich saw the untapped potential for white Christian conservative involvement in the Republican party for years prior. For two decades, he unsuccessfully tried to bait white evangelicals into political action on several issues. In 1976 however, Bob Jones University—a fundamentalist college in Greenville South Carolina—lost its tax exemption for failing to integrate. Randall Balmer chronicled his interview with one of the school's top officials, Elmer L. Rumminger. Rumminger

---

[76] Katherine Stewart, *The Power Worshippers: Inside the Dangerous Rise of Religious Nationalism* (New York, NY: Bloomsbury Publishing, 2020), 7.

[77] Jerry Falwell, interview by Bill Moyers, Moyers Moment, last modified August 31, 2012, https://billmoyers.com/content/bill-moyers-on-the-rise-of-the-religious-right/.

stated that the IRS actions against Bob Jones University "alerted the Christian school community about what could happen with government interference" in the affairs of evangelical institutions: "That was really the major issue that got us all involved."[78]

Now the attention of top evangelical leaders such as Falwell, Pat Robertson, James Dobson and others was coupled with the ideological and theological underpinnings of a lesser-known but influential Calvinist writer and theologian R.J. Rushdoony. Weyrich was finally seeing his political vision come to fruition. Though the loss of racially segregated Bob Jones University's tax exempt status was the real cause of the movement's genesis, they pivoted to adding abortion as a vital issue for the conservative cause to garner more considerable appeal and maintain momentum. Several years earlier however, abortion was mainly a Catholic issue and the evangelical response to Roe v. Wade was mostly one of acceptance. W.A. Criswell, then prominent pastor of First Baptist Church in Dallas, Texas (where Robert Jeffress currently pastors) noted at the time of the ruling: "I have always felt that it was only after a child was born and had a life separate from its mother that it became an individual person, and it has always, therefore, seemed to me that what is best for the mother and for the future should be allowed."[79] Other social issues such as same-sex marriage were also added to the conservative platform.

Even though the Religious Right has been experiencing decline, it has been a formidable political force for the Republican cause for the past four decades. They helped to elect four Republican presidential candidates in the hope that their ethno-religious vision for America would be realized. Within that time, abortion has remained a legal medical procedure, and same-sex marriage has recently been upheld

---

[78] Randall Balmer, "The Real Origins of the Religious Right," *Politico*, May 27, 2014, https://www.politico.com/magazine/story/2014/05/religious-right-real-origins-107133.

[79] Samuel P. Perry, *Rhetorics of Race and Religion on the Christian Right: Barack Obama and the War on Terror* (Lanham, MD: Lexington Books, 2020), xxiii.

by the U.S. Supreme Court. The Religious Right has expended much of their perceived political capital in service to Christian Nationalism. And yet, in the midst of their current power affair with Donald Trump, their dream of a "Christian Nation" is as elusive and illusory as it has ever been, and their prophetic witness severely compromised.

## "You will be like God"

In Genesis 3, when the snake approached Eve in the Garden of Eden and told her, "you will be like God," it was more than just an attempt to entice humanity to sin. It was an all-out assault on humanity's very identity. This was achieved by convincing them that they were not who God already created them to be. They were already like God, made in His image.[80]

Herein lies the deception and danger of the "fake news" behind Christian nationalism and its subsequent apostasy: It demands its beholder place an unnecessary onus on *becoming* that which they already are. The seeds of the great falling away are sown anytime humanity is more enamored with what they can create themselves into than the greatness they already possess. Instead of resting and living in the identity of "a holy nation" already,[81] Christians under the spell of a nationalist ideology become inordinately consumed with building their own "Tower of Babel." This involves trading in their eternal heritage and home for a temporal lineage and land.

Christian nationalism causes a Christian to forget they are on a pilgrimage and instead build a settlement, relying on human efforts to engage in unnecessary and unholy wars and alliances to protect and promote what they perceive is their "Manifest Destiny." Jesus told Pilate that "My kingdom is not from this world. If my kingdom were from this world, my followers would be fighting to keep me from being

---

[80] Gen. 1:26-27
[81] 1 Pet. 2:9.

handed over to the Jews. But as it is, my kingdom is not from here."[82] The question that remains then is, when Christians find themselves engaged in any kind of war, cultural or otherwise: whose kingdom is being promoted?

Now, this is not to say Christians should not speak up for the voiceless or take up the cause of those who have no defense. However, before the Christian engages in any fight that is perceived to be on the horizon, there needs to be a thorough assessment of the real enemy's identity. Christian nationalism always obfuscates this point for its adherents. If Paul's reminder to the Ephesians still applies today,[83] Christian nationalism has no biblical backing as a viable ideology for God's people. It always focuses people—fellow humans—as the opposition by pushing forth an "us vs. them" narrative. It never leads its adherents to appropriate conclusions about the root causes of any of their problems. So where do we go from here? What can the Black church do to escape and shield from the threat of Christian nationalism within its ranks? The Black church's own theological history offers some suggestions I deem helpful.

## "God is a Negro" – Too

Henry McNeal Turner, an African Methodist Episcopal bishop in late 19th century, uttered the words "God is a Negro" in a sermon in 1895. There was significant resistance, most notably from Henry Lyman Morehouse, a white Baptist minister and Morehouse College namesake, who stated: "Our God is not a God of any nationality, or any race, but of the whole human family; and as to color—God is a Spirit to be worshipped by renewed spirits in whatever colored bodies for a time they tabernacle of earth."[84] While on the surface Morehouse

---

[82] Jn. 18:36; this passage is taken from the NRSV.
[83] Eph. 6:12.
[84] Henry Lyman Morehouse, "The Spirit and Policy of the American Baptist Home Mission Society in its Work For the Colored People of the South," in *Baptist Home Mission Monthly* 17.11, 412-22 (1895): 414.

spoke truthfully, it nevertheless misses the point of Turner's truth. Turner would provide further clarity for "God is a Negro" in an editorial 3 years later:

> Every race of people since time began who have attempted to describe their God by words, or by paintings, or by carvings, or by any other form or figure have conveyed the idea that the God who made them and shaped their destinies was symbolized in themselves, and why should not the Negro believe that he resembles God as much as other people? We do not believe that there is any hope for a race of people who do not believe that they look like God.[85] (emphasis mine)

This statement, the last sentence in particular, I believe encapsulates the spirit behind Turner's "God is a Negro" sermon. It is a monumental attempt to affirm Blackness in a way that is faithful to God's intention for humanity when He declared: "Let us make humankind in our image, in the likeness of ourselves."[86] Andre Johnson, in describing Turner's statement as an example of "rhetorical theology," says:

> By calling God a Negro, Turner means not to engage in a systematic treatment of the Godhead or extrapolate a theoretical concept of God's nature. Rather, Turner responds to the contextual reality facing him and other African-Americans during his time, namely, how do Black people authentically serve a God in which they cannot see themselves? Image is important and how one constructs God will have an impact on how a person sees herself or himself.[87]

---

[85] Paul Harvey, *Through the Storm, Through the Night: A History of African American Christianity* (Lanham, MD: Roman and Littlefield Publishing, 2011), 165.

[86] Gen. 1:26

[87] Andre E. Johnson, "God is a Negro: The (Rhetorical) Black Theology of Bishop Henry McNeal Turner," in *Black Theology: An International Journal* 13.1, 29-40 (2015): 38.

Now I believe that Johnson is correct in his assessment of Turner's intentions. Therefore, in light of this, and of Morehouse's critique, I would like to make a slight, yet important modification to Turner's initial thesis: God is a Negro – *too*. This would be more helpful to the continuation of the Black church's formation of a distinct theology for both liberation and healing.

It is understandable that the level of oppression that Turner and African-Americans as a whole were suffering at the hands of Whites would not allow Turner any room to admit that God could also be represented in Whiteness. In fact, it could be argued he said it the way it needed to be said for his time. Nevertheless, for the Black church to continue formulating a theology that does not result in the oppressed behaving in the same manner as the oppressor and thus falling into the trap of Christian nationalism, it is essential for a people to assert their own identity in God without nullifying another's, regardless of whether they are behaving as if they were made in His image. Hence, God is a Negro – too.

Declaring that God is a Negro, too, strikes the necessary balance of asserting the Black identity in the God-narrative and preventing the dangerous descent into Black supremacy and religious nationalism of any kind. One of the early Black Christian Nationalist voices was Albert B. Cleage, Jr. Cleage opens the first chapter of his treatise on Black Christian Nationalism asserting that "generations of Black Christians have found inspiration in the tale of Israel's escape from bondage in Egypt without realizing that the Biblical Nation Israel was a Black Nation."[88] He then justifies this assertion by positing that any white Jews that exist were converts after the destruction of the Jerusalem temple in 70 CE. Setting aside that the very concept of Whiteness did not exist in 70 CE (it is a fairly recent construct in world history), the argument that Ancient Israel was a Black nation in the

---

[88] Albert B. Cleage, Jr., *Black Christian Nationalism: New Directions for the Black Church* (New York, NY: William Morrow and Company, Inc., 1972), 3.

same way Blackness is understood today is an example of Whitehead and Perry's definition of Christian nationalism. There is a reliance on myth and creative narrative for the crafting of a false and fragile identity that understandably seeks to make sense of the suffering and injustices endured by Black people.

Black people do not have to share some special link to Ancient Israel to be valued and affirmed by God. In an attempt to establish a link where there possibly is none, Black Christian Nationalism actually misses all of the ways God and the Bible affirm Blackness and identify with the unique suffering of Black people in history and to this very day. The prophecy to Cush in Isaiah 18 and its subsequent fulfillment found in the Ethiopian eunuch in Acts 8 serve as one of many pieces of evidence of a Black presence in the Bible that does not just shout "God is a Negro" but declares and affirms that God is a Negro, too. Black people are not invisible to God, and we do not have to become something we are not to obtain some special attention or access from Him other than what we already possess as His image-bearers. That is indeed good news.

Declaring "God is a Negro, too" has the potential to ground Black people that would engage in nationalist ideologies within the context of the sufferings and injustices endured by all oppressed peoples. To borrow insight from the Apostle Peter, Black people are not to "be surprised at the fiery ordeal that has come on [us] to test [us], as though something strange were happening to [us]."[89] Keeping the commonality of human suffering in view, that our "brothers and sisters in all the world are undergoing the same kinds of suffering,"[90] helps us steer clear of engaging in an exceptionalism that falsely exalts our tribulation over another for the purpose of deriving worth and value.

"God is a Negro, too" invites us to look at our would-be oppressor as our brother, and not our enemy. As stated before, Christian

---

[89] 1 Pet. 4:12.
[90] 1 Pet 5:9 taken from the NRSV.

nationalism, and nationalism in general, creates an "us vs. them" narrative that is crucial to the building of said nation. In that same vein, Cleage, in defining the "them" for Black Christian Nationalists does not lean on dehumanization, a popular tactic to which other Black religious nationalist movements have resorted. Rather, he purports that "the white man…is neither a devil or a beast, but a power-crazy individualist who can be dealt with and defeated in struggle."[91]

While it is to be commended that Cleage does not overtly dehumanize who he deems to be the enemy, there is a sort of humanity that is denied in the process of merely marking someone for active opposition. There is no room to affirm the image of God on either side. In viewing other human beings as the enemy, we forfeit the mission and ministry of reconciliation to God to which we have been called and become as bestial as those whom we have accused of being to us.[92] "God is a Negro, too" reminds us that we do not have to return animosity to appeal for accountability. What Turner declared a century ago was only the beginning of asserting Black identity and affirming the worth of Black life in the eyes of the Creator. That work must continue, especially keeping in mind the aim of the Creator to reconcile all things to Himself and our part in that mission, even in the midst of our oppression and suffering.

## Conclusion

Christian Nationalism is historically and presently detrimental to the prophetic witness of God's people. It has influenced the formation of an entire voting bloc that has for the last 40 plus years voted against its own and regular U.S. citizens' interests. This is in favor of an Antichrist ideology that superficially speaks to Christian values while undermining and abandoning the very core and identity of the

---

[91] Cleage, *Black Christian Nationalism,* 101.
[92] 2 Cor. 5:16-21.

Christian faith. Christian Nationalism has proven to be, and still is, one of the most prominent forms of apostasy. By their actions, its adherents assert that Jesus did not come in the flesh to show us the way and that it is up to us to build our own way to God. Nevertheless, the Black church can take steps to avoid and be vigilant when elements of this worldview take root among her ranks. She must continue to create a balanced identity and Gospelist theology that heals all within its grasp and does not deny anyone's right to express their worship to and call from God fully.

The Black Church must continue to develop Gospel theology in a distinctive, yet non-reactionary fashion. She must have at its heart the sentiment of Adam Small, when speaking of Blackness as an identity not formed by white responsiveness: "The primary form of expression shall be the manifestation of our blackness. Over and over again we shall make our blackness visible. We do not exist for the benefit of the whites. We *exist*."[93] And it is in that daring to exist, and not to justify its existence, that the Black Church shall continue to find its strength to fulfill the greatest commandment.[94] Martin Luther King, Jr. shares an insight he received from his mother during his formative years that shaped his life in a monumental way, and it seems also to be helpful for the Black Church:

> My mother confronted the age-old problem of the Negro parent in America: how to explain discrimination and segregation to a small child. She taught me that I should feel a sense of "somebodiness" but that on the other hand I had to go out and face a system that stared me in the face every day saying you are "less than," you are "not equal to." She told me about slavery and how it ended with the Civil War. She tried

---

[93] Allan Boesak, *Black and Reformed: Apartheid, Liberation, and the Calvinist Tradition* (Eugene, OR: Wipf & Stock, 2015), 7.
[94] Mt. 22:37-40.

to explain the divided system of the South—the segregated schools, restaurants, theaters, housing; the white and colored signs on drinking fountains, waiting rooms, lavatories—as a social condition rather than a natural order. She made it clear that she opposed this system and that I must never allow it to make me feel inferior. Then she said the words that almost every Negro hears before he can yet understand the injustice that makes them necessary: "You are as good as anyone."[95]

Turner's statement, while radical and controversial even to this day, carries a spirit behind it that the Black Church can find helpful. The Black church can continue to exude a greater level of confidence and assurance that she *too* reflects God's image as she deals with those entities and institutions that seek to denigrate, ignore, and subjugate. Turner's words, slightly modified to "God is a Negro – too," ought to further encourage a greater spirit of appreciation and consideration within the Black church as they interact with one another as God's children. They also teach the Black church to foster a balanced, grounded sense of worth and value for herself and those that would oppress her, as she walks out God's mission to reconcile the world to Himself.

---

[95] Martin Luther King, *The Autobiography of Martin Luther King, Jr*, ed. by Clayborne Carson (New York, NY: IPM, 2001), 3-4.

# Rit'at of Ag'azi: Patristic Visions of Black Orthodoxy

### Vince L. Bantu

Black, academic theology has primarily been carried out in white institutions and through white theological frameworks. White conservative theology has historically and at present is largely on the wrong side of justice issues. White liberal theology is heretical in its pluralism but has given better lip-service to justice issues and, therefore, has attracted more Black scholars to their institutions. The majority of Black theological scholarship in the academy has followed the suit of their white theological educators in many respects. One aspect of Black liberal academic theology is a tendency to reject the very concept of "orthodoxy"—or correct, life-giving belief—as a product of white people.[97] Consider the following remarks from the founder of liberal, academic Black theology:

> It is all right to say as did Athanasius that the Son is *homoousia* (one substance with the Father), especially if one has a taste for Greek philosophy and a feel for the importance of intellectual distinctions. And I do not want to minimize or detract from the significance of Athanasius' assertion for faith one iota.

---

[96] I am grateful to Dr. Aaron Butts for his helpful comments and guidance on this study.
[97] Bruce L. Fields, *Introducing Black Theology: Three Crucial Questions for the Evangelical Church* (Eugene, OR: Wipf and Stock Publishers, 2001), 50.

But the *homoousia* question is not a black question. Blacks do not ask whether Jesus is one with the Father or divine and human, though the orthodox formulations are implied in their language.[98]

I affirm Cone's critique of the white theological academy's tendency to ignorantly present white theology and ministry practices as normative. I also partially affirm Cone's central thesis that social context influences the questions a community forms about Tilli (Nub: God). I use the word "influence" here as a contrast to Cone's claim that social context "decides" a community's questions about Tilli. Indeed, Cone goes on to claim that Athanasius' concern for the full divinity of Jesus was based in his desire for "intellectual distinctions" that were based in his Greek philosophical background that was devoid from situations of oppression and slavery. On this point, Cone is straight trippin'. Athanasius was himself an African theologian of color who lived in a community that was colonized and enslaved by the Roman Empire and he experienced exile for his orthodoxy. Athanasius stood in the company of many other African theologians in Egypt, Nubia and Ag'azi (Ethiopia) who defended and died for rit'at. Cone's claim that the question of Jesus' divinity is not a "black question" is historically inaccurate, theologically heretical and psychologically oppressive. Black Nazrawis (Eth: Christian)—ancient and modern—have been deeply concerned with denouncing heresy and proclaiming rit'at ("orthodoxy"). Following white thinking, Black liberal theologians have bifurcated belief from practice and then prioritized the latter over the former. The following paper will explore the development of orthodoxy—or rit'at—in the context of the Christianization of the first Black Nazrawi nation: Ethiopia, or as it was known to its original inhabitants, Ag'azi. I will further demonstrate that embracing right

---

[98] James H. Cone, *God of the Oppressed* (Maryknoll, NY: Orbis Books, 1975), 18-19.

belief and avoiding wrong belief is a value that has been among Black folk from day one.

## Rit'at in the Court of the Neguś

Ag'azi embraced the Bisrat (Eth: "Gospel") as its national religion in the fourth century under the neguś (Eth: "king") Ezana. Material evidence indicates that Ezana—much like King Silko of Nubia—experienced a gradual conversion to the Bisrat.[99] Today the most well-known archaeological site in Axum is the field of imperial, funerary obelisks. The tallest of these is commonly associated with King Ezana and is adorned at the top with an image to the sun—the focal point of pre-Nazrawi worship.[100] Also located in Axum is a trilingual, imperial tablet, which narrates Ezana's victory over the Kushite Beja and was recorded in Sabean, Ge'ez and Greek scripts.[101] One of the earliest Ge'ez inscriptions, often known by Western scholars as the *Monumentum Adulitanum*, claimed that the kingdom of Ag'azi extended as far as "the borders of the Egyptian territory (τῆς Αἰγύπτου ὁρίων οἰκοῦντα)."[102] One of the several Ezana stelea, written in Greek, bears witness to various African people groups, some of which are otherwise

---

[99] For discussion on the Christianization of Nubia and King Silko, see Salim Faraji, *The Roots of Nubian Christianity Uncovered: The Triumph of the Last Pharaoh* (Trenton, NJ: Africa World Press, 2012).

[100] E.A. Wallis Budge, *A History of Ethiopia, Vol. II* (New York, NY: Routledge, 2014), 625.

[101] Bowersock points out the numismatic evidence illustrating the common practice for late antique Axum deploying Greek and Ge'ez inscriptions, Glen W. Bowersock, *The Throne of Adulis: Red Sea Wars on the Eve of Islam* (Oxford: Oxford University Press, 2013), 70; such stelae may have been modelled after trilingual Persian boundary markers that were less intended to be read in Greek but to serve diplomatic functions, Stephanie L. Black, "'In the Power of God Christ': Greek Inscriptional Evidence for the Anti-Arian Theology of Ethiopia's First Christian King," in *BSOAS* 71, 93-110 (2008): 94.

[102] Cosmas Indicopleustes, *Christian Topography*, ed. E.O. Winstedt (Cambridge: Cambridge University Press, 1909), 62; at this time, the Meroitic Kushite kingdom was in decline, Angelika Lohwasser, "Das 'Ende von Meroe': Gedanken zur Regoinalität von Ereignissen," in *Ägypten und sein Umfeld in der Spätantike. Vom Regierungsantritt Diokletians 284/285 bis zur arabischen Eroberung des Vorderen Orients um 635-646. Aketen der Tagung vom 7.-9.7.2011 in Münster*, 275-290 (Wiesbaden: Harrassowitz, 2013), 279.

unknown. Various such people groups are reported to be subjects of Ezana's empire: "I Ezanas, King of the Axumites (Ἀξωμιτῶν) and Himyarites (Ὁμηριτῶν) and of Reeidan (ΡΕΕΙΔΑΝ) and the Sabeans (Σαβαειτῶν) and of Sileel (ΣΙΛΕΗΛ) and of Khasoa (ΧΑΣΩ) and the Bejas (Βουγαειτῶν) and of Tiamo (Τιαμῶ), Bisi Alene, son of Elle-Amida, a servant of Christ."[103] This stele claims that the neguś of Agʻazi went to war against the Nubians in response to appeals for aid from neighboring African communities: "I went out to wage war with the Noba (ΝΩΒΑ), because the Mangartho (ΜΑΝΓΑΡΘΩ) and Khasa (ΧΑΣΑ) and Atiaditai (ΑΤΙΑΔΙΤΑΙ) and Bareotai (ΒΑΡΕΩΤΑΙ) told us as they cried out: 'The Noba have oppressed us. Help us, because they have oppressed us by killing us!'"[104] Indeed, Egyptian Demotic sources attest to the conflicts between the Nubians and a neighboring nomadic group known alternatively as Blemmyes/Beja: "In the year in question the Blemmyes (*Ble.w*) had gone against the Nubians (*Nwbe.w*). They had handed over hostages in regnal year 90 of Diocletian."[105] But peep game on how the stela indicates that it was out of protection for various African ethnic groups that Ezana went to war against Nubia. And then peep how the stela calls Ezana a "servant of Christ" (δοῦλος χριστοῦ). The stela represents that at the beginning of the Agʻazi Nazrawi tradition, the values of ritʻat and justice were promoted at the highest levels of society. The authors of the imperial stelae sought to communicate a concern for surrounding oppressed Africans and to depict their neguś as a "servant of Christ." This is indicative of an ancient African tradition that developed autonomously from Greco-Roman Christendom and promoted the value of doctrinal correctness of its own accord.

---

[103] Black, "In the Power of God Christ," 101.
[104] Black, "In the Power of God Christ," 102.
[105] Jitse H.F. Dijkstra, *Religious Encounters on the Southern Egyptian Frontier in Late Antiquity (AD298-642)* (Ph.D. diss.: University of Gronnigen, 2005), 43.

However, the nature of the haymanot (Eth: "faith") of Ezana remains unclear. This is evident in one of the other multi-lingual, imperial stela commissioned by Ezana. Like the Silko inscription at Kalabsha, Ezana attributes his victory to a monotheistic God and depicts himself as His divine agent: "And I dedicated this stela and consecrated it to heaven and earth and the Creator, the invincible Ares. If anyone desires to harm them, may the God of Heaven and Earth (ὁ θεὸς τοῦ οὐρανοῦ καὶ τῆς γῆς) completely destroy him, and may his name on the earth of the living no longer exist."[106] It is likely that Ezana maintained pre-Nazrawi religious behavior while promoting and supporting the ministry of the Urpeh (Coptic: "Church") in a gradual Christianization of Ethiopia.[107] The unvocalized Ge'ez translation dedicates Ezana's victory "to *'str, bḥr* and *mḥrm*," ( ⵍⵓⵙⵜⵣ ⵡⴱⵃⵣ ⵡⵍⵎⵃⵣⵎ)[108] names of pre-Christian Axumite deities. The Greek side of this inscription quoted above gives praise to the Greek god Ares. This indicates the syncretistic nature of Ezana's haymanot that embraced indigenous Axumite, Sabean and Greek pagan religion as well as the Bisrat.

However, the other imperial inscription commissioned by Ezana already quoted above relates the same military victory in unequivocally

---

[106] Siegert Uhlig, "Eine trilinguale 'Ezana-Inschrift," in *Aethiopica* 4, 7-31 (2001): 19; all translations of non-English, ancient sources have been done by the author.

[107] David W. Phillipson, *Foundations of an African Civilisation: Aksum and the Northern Horn, 1000 BC – AD 1300* (Addis Ababa: Addis Ababa University Press, 2012), 96. Hatke argues that Ezana was likely Christian by the time of Athanasius' treatise regarding Constantius but that it may have been later that Ezana embraced orthodox (Nicene) Christianity, George Hatke *Aksum and Nubia: Warfare, Commerce, and Political Fictions in Ancient Northeast Africa* (New York, NY: New York University Press, 2013), 94.

[108] Uhlig, "Eine trilinguale 'Ezana-Inschrift," 23; Piovanelli suggests that Ezana's older brother and predecessor Ousanas (reign c. 320 CE) may have been on the gradual road to Christian conversion based on the numismatic Axumite tendency to remove traditional religious imagery from coinage, Pierluigi Piovanelli, "Social and Cultural History of the Axumite Kingdom," in *Inside and Out: Interactions between Rome and the Peoples on the Arabian and Egyptian Frontiers in Late Antiquity*, eds. Jitse H.F. Dijkstra & Greg Fisher, 331-352 (Leuven: Peeters, 2014), 349.

Nazrawi language: "By faith in God and by the power of the Father and Son and Holy Spirit, to the one who saved the kingship (βασίλιον) for me by faith in his son Jesus Christ."[109] Such explicitly Nazrawi language is only evident on the Greek side of the imperial stelae, while the Geʻez inscription renders praise to Greek gods. This indicates the syncretistic belief of Ezana and the religious diversity of fourth-century Agʻazi.[110] However, given the clearly Nazrawi nature of the haymanot on the Greek side of the inscription, a genuine Nazrawi in the court of Ezana is the most likely author. The ritiʻt ("orthodox") language in the stela indicates that, while Ezana likely may have held a syncretistic religious belief system, ritiʻt Nazrawi inhabited fourth-century Agʻazi at various social levels.

It is noteworthy that, even centuries after the Christianization of Agʻazi, remnants of pre-Nazrawi religion persisted. In one of the rock-hewn uprehs of Lalibela—Bete Mariam (Church of Mary)—an icon of the sun rests beside several typical Nazrawi icons, contextualizing Nazrawi iconography in the context of Agʻazi.[111] This connects with the Gospel Haymanot value of sankofa. The presence of sun veneration in Agʻazi Nazrawi practice demonstrates the degree to which the Agʻazi "went back and got" the traditions of their ancestors and contextualized them in agreement with the Bisrat. This is like white Christians who have fused their pre-Christian, Anglo-Saxon practices such as Christmas trees and Easter. Therefore, in Agʻazi visions of ritʻat, the proclamation of right belief is neither beholden to white framing nor antithetical to African cultural values.

---

[109] Black, "'In the Power of God Christ,'" 101.
[110] Piovanelli, "Social and Cultural History," 349.
[111] Vince L. Bantu, *A Multitude of All Peoples: Engaging Ancient Christianity's Global Identity* (Downers Grove, IL: InterVarsity Press Academic, 2020), 104.

## The Rit'at of Fremanatos

It has been argued that John Chrysostom believed that the Agʻazi were present at the coming of the Holy Spirit at Pentecost and that Rufinus of Aquileia understood the apostle Matthew to have been chosen by lot to evangelize "Ethiopia."[112] While it is possible that Christianity first came to Agʻazi in the first century—especially given the high degree of contact with the Eastern Roman Empire through the Red Sea maritime trade—the earliest historically substantiated Nazrawi period in Agʻazi was under the fourth-century Neguś Ezana. The Roman historian Rufinus relates that two young Syrian brothers—Aedesius and Frumentius—came to Agʻazi from Tyre with their merchant uncle Meropius. Upon arrival, their ship was attacked and all but the two youths were killed. Rufinus' account provides a sample of the Roman attitude towards Ethiopians: "It is the custom of the barbarians there (*moris est inibi barbarorum*) that whenever the neighboring people groups report that partnership with the Romans has been disturbed, they kill all the Romans they find among them."[113]

Rufinus' Roman bias is evident throughout his account as he credits Frumentius' missionary success in Agʻazi to other Roman Christian merchants who introduced the Bisrat to the Agʻazi. This likely indicates Rufinus' strategy of connecting the evangelization of "outlying" territories to the Roman Christian "center," as the historian would have perceived it. Rufinus claims that the Roman expression of the Bisrat resulted in the mass Agʻazi converts who "flocked to the Roman custom of prayer (*Romano ritu oratinois causa confluerent*)."[114]

---

[112] Isaac, *The Ethiopian Orthodox Täwahïdo Church*, 17.

[113] Rufinus of Aquilieia, *Church History*, eds. Eduard Schwartz & Theodor Mommsen, *Die griechischen christlichen schriftsteller der ersten drei jahrhunderte: herausgegeben von der kirchenväter-comission der königl, preussischen akademie der wissenschaften: Eusebius, zweiter band, zweiter teil* (Leipzig: J.C. Hinrichs'sche Buchhandlung, 1908), 972.

[114] Rufinus, *Church History*, 972. The same Roman Christian paternalistic tone is communicated in Athanasius' recording of the letter to King Ezana from Emperor Constantius, who desires to "extend knowledge of the Almighty (κρείττονος γνῶσις)" to neighboring kingdoms, a

Athanasius similarly expresses the typical Roman attitude of viewing Axum as "the country of the barbarians (μέχρι τῆς βαρβάρων)."[115] Although Aedesius and Frumentius were enslaved under Neguś Ella Amida, the king freed them shortly before his death as they had grown in favor and reputation in the imperial court.

The widowed queen besought the brothers to serve as imperial advisors and educators for her son and future Neguś Ezana. Aedesius and Frumentius used their political influence to spread the Bisrat until Neguś Ezana came of age and allowed them to leave Ag'azi. Aedesius returned to his native Tyre while Frumentius sought out the Alexandrian Patriarch Athanasius to install a bishop over the Ag'azi Urpeh centered in Axum. Athanasius ordained Frumentius as bishop of Axum and he became the first Abuna (Eth: "father," i.e., Patriarch) of the Ethiopian Church, known also as *Abuna Salama, Kassate Berhan* ("Father of Peace, Revealer of Light"): "Then Athanasius, for he had recently received the priesthood, after closely and carefully considering the words and deeds of Frumentius, in the council of priests said: 'Can we find any other man like him? Who is God's spirit in as it is in you? Who is able to achieve such things as these?'"[116] Rufinus claims Frumentius' ordination occurred close to that of Athanasius (328 CE) while Athanasius' account in the *Apologia ad Constantinum* places the event in the mid-350s. Amidon is likely correct that Rufinus presents

---

duty which "the whole race of humanity claims from (Romans) in this matter," Athanasius of Alexandria, *Apologia ad Constantinum*, ed. Jacques-Paul Migne, *Patrologiæ Græcæ* 25, 593-642 (Paris: Imprimerie Catholique, 1857), 636.

[115] Athanasius, *Apologia ad Constantinum*, 632.

[116] Rufinus, *Church History*, 973. While this is the traditional name for Frumentius in the Ethiopian Orthodox Church, Haile argues that Frumentius and Abuna Salama are actually different people who both evangelized Axum at different periods in Late Antiquity, Getatchew Haile, "The Homily in Honour of St. Frumentius Bishop of Axum," in *Analecta Bollandiana* 97, 309-318 (1979): 313. For a more recent treatment of this dersan ("homily"), see Massimo Villa, "Frumentius in the Ethiopic Sources: Mythopoeia and Text-Critical Considerations," in *Rassegna di Studi Etiopici* 3.1 (Naples: Itituto per l'Oriente "C.A. Nallino"/Università degli Studi di Napoli "L'Orientale," 2017), 87-111.

an altered chronology in order to place the event during the reign of Constantine—whom his *Church History* holds in the highest regard.[117]

## Constantius and Arianism

Emperor Constantine's son and successor Constantius wrote a letter to Ezana requesting that Frumentius be examined by an Arian bishop in Egypt named George to confirm that his theology was "orthodox" (i.e., Arian). The letter from Constantius to Ezana survives in Athanasius' treatise against the Roman emperor *Apologia ad Constantium*, which corroborates the tradition that Frumentius was ordained as Ethiopia's first bishop by Athanasius:

> For surely you know and remember—unless that which everyone is abundantly aware of, you alone pretend to be ignorant of—that this Frumentius was ordained to his present rank (τάξιν τοῦ βίου κατέστησεν) by Athanasius, who is responsible for countless acts of wickedness; for he has not been able to justly exonerate himself of any of his charges, but was immediately deprived of his (episcopal) throne, and now he wanders completely and utterly lost, migrating from one land to another, just as if by this means he could flee his own wickedness.[118]

Constantius issued paternalistic warnings to the Neguś of Agʻazi that contain veiled threats against failing to comply with his directives: "For the concern is, lest he should cross into Auxumis and destroy your community, by setting before them polluted and accursed teachings (λόγους ἐναγεῖς καὶ δυσσεβεῖς), and not only unsettle and confuse the Churches, and blaspheme the Almighty, but also overturn and destroy each of the people groups he travels

---

[117] Philip R. Amidon, *The Church History of Rufinus of Aquilieia: Books 10 and 11* (Oxford: Oxford University Press, 1997), 47, n. 20.
[118] Athanasius, *Apologia ad Constantium*, 636.

to."[119] Much of Constantius' motivation was likely influenced by recent political gains over his rivals in the Western Roman Empire and his Persian enemies to the East.[120] By the time of the composition of the *Apologia*, Constantius was sole emperor and suppressed religious communities outside of Arian Christianity. Yet, the emperor was unable to successfully arrest Athanasius, a reality that likely caused the emperor significant frustration. The desire to spread Arian Christianity in Ag'azi would greatly aid the Roman Emperor in gaining control of the Egyptian Urpeh, which was successfully hiding their Apa (Coptic: "Patriarch"). Constantius demanded that Frumentius travel to Egypt to be examined by the Arian bishop George who had been imposed in place of the exiled Athanasius: "Now if Frumentius will immediately obey, and shall yield to an examination into all the circumstances of his ordination, it will be evident to all that he is in no respect dissonant to the laws of the Church and the dominant faith (τῆς Ἐκκλησίας νόμῳ καὶ τῇ κρατούσῃ πίστει)."[121] The pronounced anti-Arianism in the *Apologia* provides an important insight into Athanasius' strategy for narrating the evangelization of Ag'azi through the lens of the theological battle in which he was embroiled at the moment of the text's composition.

But peep game on this: at the time that Ag'azi embraced the Bisrat as a nation, the Roman Empire was under the leadership of a heretical emperor who did not believe that Jesus was Tilli (Nub: "God"). And on top of that, the heretical Roman emperor was attempting to enforce Arianism on the African Nazrawi communities in Egypt and Ag'azi. At the beginning of the Nazrawization of the first African nation, Africans were embracing rit'at while the European context was under heretical leadership. Therefore, the idea that rit'at is a

---

[119] Athanasius, *Apologia ad Constantium*, 637.
[120] Timothy Barnes, *Athanasius and Constantius: Theology and Politics in the Constantinian Empire* (Cambridge, MA: Harvard University Press, 1993), 165.
[121] Athanasius, *Apologia ad Constantium*, 636.

product of white Christendom or that matters of theological precision are unimportant to Black people are both untenable. Not only did the earliest Nazrawis in Agʻazi embrace ritiʻt haymanot, but they did so in uniquely Agʻazi ways.

Egyptian and Agʻazi Nazrawi traditions have commonly narrated a theological and ecclesiastical alignment beginning with the Patriarchs Athanasius and Frumentius.[122] However, the Ezana Inscription invoking the Silase (Eth: "Trinity") attributing Agʻazi's victory to the "power of God Christ" (τῇ δυνάμι τοῦ θεοῦ χριστοῦ), a decidedly anti-Arian phrase, indicates ritiʻt haymanot predominating fourth-century Agʻazi.[123] While the genitive case both of θεοῦ ("God") and χριστοῦ ("Christ") could hypothetically indicate a possessive construction (i.e., "the God of Christ"), all translators of this inscription have not understood the construction this way and have rendered χριστοῦ as modifying θεοῦ attributively, thus "God, that is Christ".[124]

## Agʻazi and Roman Sources on the Provenance of Ritʻat

The introduction of ritiʻt haymanot into Agʻazi during the Axumite period did not occur in a top-down manner from the imperial court only. Indeed, the anonymous author of the Geʻez dersan (Eth: "homily") on Frumentius notes that the Syrian missionary found Nazrawis present when he set out on his missionary work:

---

[122] The testimony of Athanasius that Constantius addressed a letter to Ezana, king of Axum, serves as sufficient evidence to corroborate the association of the fourth-century Axumite monarch with the missionary Frumentius. Bowersock's doubt in this regard, therefore, seems unwarranted, Bowersock, *Throne of Adulis*, 74.

[123] Black, "'In the Power of God Christ,'" 101; Piovanelli, "Social and Cultural History," 349.

[124] Black, "In the Power of God Christ," 107; see also, Anfray, Caquot and Nautin's rendering of θεοῦ χριστοῦ as "Dieu Christ," Francis Anfray, André Caquot & Pierre Nautin, "Une nouvelle inscription grecque d'Ezana, roi d'Axoum," in *Journal des savants*, 260-274 (1970:4): 266

Freminatos fervently inquired about haymanot (ሃይማኖት), and having searched for Christians in the marketplace, he found them. Then he reported to them everything that happened and he asked them to go to a quiet place so that they might sing songs. And every opportunity they had to learn, they spent the days doing so. And they built a house of prayer as they taught and trained many of us and they gathered to themselves many of the Agʻazi (አግዓዚ) people.[125]

Peep how the dersan says that there were already Nazrawis in Agʻazi before Frumentius began his ministry! Now this text claims that it came later than the fourth-century report of Rufinus. While the manuscript in which this dersan has been preserved is from the fourteenth century, it likely originated during the Axumite period of Agʻazi history (4th-10th cent.).[126] Agʻazi sources paint a different picture than Greek sources do. Notice how the Roman historian Rufinus both attributes the emergence of the Bisrat in Agʻazi to the reign of Constantine and incorrectly refers to Agʻazi as "Further India":

> In the division of the earth which—for the preaching of God's Word—the apostles enacted by lot, when the different provinces (*provinciae*) fell it is said the lot decreed that to Thomas (fell) Parthia, to Matthew (fell) Ethiopia (*Aethiopia*), and Hither India (*citerior India*), which adjoins it, (fell) to Bartholomew. Between this (province) and Parthia, but far inland, is Further India (*India ulterior*). Many language and people groups reside

---

[125] Haile, "Homily," 315. The reference to finding Christians is unique to this dersan, calling into question the claim that the dersan "slavishly follows the account of Socrates Scholasticus, Villa, "Frumentius in the Ethiopic Sources," 93. Rather, the dersan's unique claim of Nazrawis preceding the ministry of Frumentius is absent in Socrates and Rufinus and stands as a significant claim about African Nazrawi history.

[126] Haile, "Homily," 311; it is of note that the name "Ethiopia" is not used in the dersan, but the original name Agʻazi. This likely indicates that the dersan was written during the Axumite period as the name "Ethiopia" was adopted after this period.

(there), it so far away that the plow of the apostolic preaching had made no impression, but in Constantine's time it received the first seeds of faith.[127]

While Greek sources depict Frumentius as the initiator of the Nazrawi faith in Axum, Agʻazi sources understand Frumentius as the first bishop who brought ecclesiastical structure to an already present Nazrawi community. Therefore, Frumentius should not be seen as the bringer of the Bisrat to Agʻazi but as an important participant in its development which was already underway before his arrival. This further indicates the spread of the Bisrat among various levels of society. While the neguś and his imperial court were embracing the Bisrat at the top, Nazrawi were also present in the marketplace gathering for worship among the working class.

Geography was not the only misleading aspect of the Roman account of Agʻazi's evangelization. Rufinus deliberately misconstrued the timeline of events to have it appear that the Christianization of Ethiopia occurred during the reign of Constantine—the pride of Christian Rome—rather than the heretic Constantius.[128] Rufinus' narration of the missionary work of Frumentius influenced Roman Christian historians that followed him. Socrates Scholasticus

---

[127] Rufinus, *Church History*, 971-972; it was typical among ancient Greek historians to refer to "Ethiopia" and "India" interchangeably, Cosmas, *Christian Topography*, 62. "Inner India" is sometimes referred to as "Barbaria," a region understood to lie where "the land of the Ethiopians ends" (ἡ γῆ Αἰθιοτίας τέλος ἔχει). However, at times Cosmas conflates the two: "Ham and his progeny (received) the environs in the west, the so-called Gadeira, as far as the ocean of Ethiopia, called Barbaria (τοῦ Ὠκεανοῦ τῆς Αἰθιοπίας τῆς καλοθμένης βαρβαρίας), well beyond the Arabian Gulf," 61. The second-century Nicomedian historian Arrian also differentiates between the groups in his account of the conquests of Alexander: "They (Indians) were blacker than the rest of people, except the Ethiopians (μελαντέρους τῶν ἄλλων ἀνθρώπων, πλὴν Αἰθιότων); and in war they were by far the noblest of all the inhabitants of Asia at that time," Arrian of Nicomedia, *Anabasis of Alexander*, ed. C. Sintenis (Leipzig: Weidmannsche Buchhandlung, 1849), 67. The Roman understanding of "Ethiopian" geography therefore, was unclear and inconsistent.

[128] Amidon, *The Church History*, 47, n. 20. See also, Françoise Thelamon, "Rufin historien de son temps," *AAAd* 31 (1987), 1.41-59.

reiterates the same course of events, stating his reliance on Rufinus' conversation with Adesius. Socrates' description of the apostolic assignment of mission supports the idea of "Ethiopia" and "Hither India" as references to Nubian (Cushite) kingdoms:

> For at that time the peoples both of the inland Indians (Ἰωδῶν τε τῶν ἐωδοτέρω), and of the Iberians, first embraced Christianity, but regarding the one additional phrase "inland" (τῶν ἐνδοτέρω), it would be useful to briefly explain. When the apostles journeyed by lot among the peoples, Thomas received the apostleship of the Parthians; Matthew that of Ethiopia; and Bartholomew was allotted the part of India connected (συνημμένην) to that country; but inland India, which was inhabited by many barbarous peoples with various colorful languages, was not enlightened (ἐφώτιζε) by Christian doctrine before the time of Constantine.[129]

Language biased in favor of Rome persisted also in the account of the church historian Theodoret of Cyrrhus who credited the conversion of many nations during the fourth century as rooted in a desire to be at peace with Rome. Theodoret reported that "at this time (reign of Constantine), the light of the knowledge of God (θεογνωσίας) was brought forth to India...A foreign philosopher from Tyre, searching from a desire to obtain to further India (ἐσχάτην Ἰωδίαν), set out with his two young nephews."[130] Upon receiving ordination from Athanasius, the account of Theodoret states that Frumentius "returned to the uncivilized people (ἀγεώργητον ἔθνος)" of the "Indians."[131] This kind of Romano-centric language laid the foundation for false ideas that

---

[129] Socrates Scholasticus, *Ecclesiastical History*, ed. William Bright (Oxford: Clarendon Press, 1893), 39.
[130] Theodoret, *Historia Ecclesiastica*, 969.
[131] Theodoret, *Historia Ecclesiastica*, 972.

Christianity and orthodoxy come from the Roman (and later, Western/white) world. However, African sources paint a different picture.

Sources relating the evangelization of Ethiopia who travelled the land or had close ecclesiastical ties with the earliest Axumite Church provide more accurate geographical descriptors for Frumentius' missionary activity. It is not surprising then, that Athanasius used the name "Axum" (Αὐξούμεως)[132] in reference to Frumentius' bishopric; while Rufinus—and subsequent Roman historians—placed Frumentius in "Hither India," and understood "Ethiopia" to reside in a completely different region altogether. Roman historians further removed from Ethiopian Christian activity relied on constructions of "Ethiopia" and "India" that confuse the location of an otherwise informative account of the evangelization of Ethiopia.

However, Ag'azi sources de-emphasize Roman imperial nomenclature in identifying the source of their evangelization. The Axumite dersan emphasizes the land of Tyre as the origin of their first bishop Frumentius: "And it was when he (Frumentius) was in the land of Tyre that he was appointed for the land of the Ag'aze" (wäbäbəhera ṣəra' 'ənzä halo täśäymä läbəherä 'äg'azē ወበብሔረ ጽርአ እንዘ ሀሎ ተሠይመ ለብሔረ አግዐዜ).[133] Interestingly, Ethiopian sources refer to all Roman territories as "Tyre" (ṣəra' ጽርአ) in a similar way that Roman sources label various regions south of Egypt inhabited by dark-skinned people as "Ethiopia." This anonymous Ge'ez homily even refers to Egypt as "Tyre" when the author refers to Alexandria as the location of Frumentius' ordination by Athanasius. In addition to expressing a uniquely Ag'azi topographical imagination, the dersan on Frumentius also confirms the value or

---

[132] Athanasius, *Apologia ad Constantinum*, 636.
[133] Haile, "Homily," 315. I have translated ṣəra' as "Tyre," per Haile's suggestion on p. 312, n. 2 as opposed to his translation, which renders ṣəra' as "Greece." The Ge'ez spelling of ṣəra' is much closer to "Tyre" and the usual Ge'ez word for things pertaining to Greek people and places is *yonanawi*. Villa understands ṣəra' to refer to Egypt, Villa, "Frumentius in the Ethiopic Sources," 97.

rit'at among the earliest Nazrawis. After being freed from slavery, Frumentius appealed to Athanasius, Pope of Egypt, to return as bishop of Ag'azi:

> But Freminatyos arrived at Alexandria, to Chief Pope Athanasius, who he found recently ordained. Having entered before him, he told him everything about himself—how he travelled, how he became a slave, how he found favor with the neguś (ንጉሥ), and how there was hope for the haymanot (ሃይማኖት) in Christ in the land of Ag'aze (አግዓዜ). So Freminatyos asked Chief Pope Athanasius to ordain bishops and priests and to send them to the land of Ag'aze. And imploring him, he said: "For the sake of Christ, do not neglect them so that they may receive salvation." And Chief Pope Athanasius decided that the best thing would be to ordain Freminatos himself as Pope, as he said: "There is no one that we will find who is more suitable than him." So Freminatyos was ordained as one who is worthy of the papacy. He came at once to the land of Ag'aze and became a preacher of the haymanot of Christ.[134]

Peep how the main concern among Ag'azi historiographers was the concern for rit'at among the people of Ag'azi. The principal concern of Athanasius and Frumentius as recorded by Ag'azi historians is the salvation of Ag'azi through haymanot in Jesus. The Ag'azi sources include statements of concern for salvation and haymanot in uniquely Ag'azi ways that are not present in the Greek accounts of Frumentius and Athanasius. This indicates the degree to which haymanot riti't was a universal Nazrawi principle that was expressed in contextualized ways in Ag'azi.

In the same way, the haymanot riti't expressed in the Ezana stela also expressed an orthodox understanding of the divinity of Jesus in

---

[134] Haile, "Homily," 315.

unique ways. The appellation θεοῦ χριστοῦ is an attestation unique to this stela that is not found in other orthodox Greek writers during this period. Therefore, while the imperial Nazrawi scribes working under Ezana affirmed the same rit'it faith in the full divinity of Jesus that was being espoused by Christians in the Roman Empire, they did so in a manner unique to the Nazrawis of Ag'azi.

## Conclusion

Liberal, academic theology done by Black scholars has been predominately characterized by an increasing tendency to de-emphasize the importance of haymanot riti't. The liberationist and womanist theological paradigms invented during the Cone generation elevated the aspects of the Shajeh (Bible) that advocate for social liberation while ignoring passages that call for exclusive faith in Jesus the Messiah. Contemporary liberal, Black academic theology has pushed this further and has called into question the need for the Shajeh or even Tilli in theological discourse. Much of the work of theologian Anthony Pinn has focused on white questions such as theodicy and has provided answers framed in white paradigms such as humanism while presenting such theology as "African-American":

> African American nontheistic humanist theology has no sacred texts in a traditional sense because it pays no allegiance to the idea of revealed materials that link the transcendent and human history. The Hebrew Bible and the Christian scriptures have some metaphorical or symbolic value through their teaching of both positive and negative life lessons, and to the extent this is the case, nontheistic theology understands them to offer source material for theologizing humanism. However, these books are read devoid of any sense that they contain some form of revelation from cosmic forces, and highlighted… instead is the appeal to humanistic frameworks lodged in these

storybooks. Furthermore, these texts and their insights are no more significant and hold no greater meaning than what one gathers, for example, from the literary imaginings of figures such as Richard Wright and Toni Morrison...While the theology outlined in this volume gives no special attention to the Christian tradition, unlike black and womanist theologies, it does share their concern with African American experience and history as theological source materials. Yet, it does not read these through the Christ Event as pointing toward the outcome of salvation history. Rather, African American experience and history are mined for what they say about humanist sensibilities and practices. In a word, these materials are all viewed for how they explicate the humanist tradition.[135]

Pinn proffers an African-American theology that can do without the Urpeh, the Shajeh, even Tilli. The Greek concept of "theology" means "talk" or "discourse" about "Tilli." Yet Pinn's view of theology is one that does not necessarily need Tilli. I got love for the brother and his commitment to the community but he trippin on this one. How you gon have theology without Tilli? For Pinn, the human condition and experience is the primary source and object of theology. By centering his vision of African-American theology in humanism, Pinn has placed the African-American theological experience under the umbrella of a white, European philosophical framework. This might work in academic contexts, but Black folks in the hood have experienced too much oppression and know better than to place faith in our own human ability to achieve our own flourishing. Black folk know that there is a Tilli that is with us. Despite the injustice and oppression that exists in the world because of our rejection of His Law, Tilli is still working all injustices meant for our harm into good. While the Greek term "discourse" about

---

[135] Anthony B. Pinn, *The End of God-Talk: An African American Humanist Theology* (Oxford: Oxford University Press, 2012), 9.

Tilli refers primarily to the action of talking, the ancient African concept of haymanot refers not simply to talk about Tilli, but a wholistic faith that is spoken, believed and lived. In this way, the African value of haymanot riti'it has been a core element of Black theology centuries before humanism was invented by white philosophers. The first generation of liberal, Black academic theology subordinated the concept of rit'at to the value of social liberation while also dismissing the concept of theological orthodoxy as a product of white, Western values. There is now a trend in the current generation of liberal, Black academic theology to not only reject theological orthodoxy but the Shajeh and Tilli as well. Considering Tilli as a dispensable factor subordinate to human flourishing is a very white way of thinking and is foreign to the majority of African and African-descended worldviews.

The value of rit'at has been among Black people from day one. The Ge'ez language is one of the oldest sub-Saharan languages in the world and one of the language's first inscriptions proclaims the orthodox belief that Jesus is Tilli. Truth, orthodoxy and life-saving faith is indeed a Black concern. Like other members of the global Body of Christ, Black Nazrawis around the world have historically held firmly to the truth that Jesus is the only Lord and Savior of the world. This is still the belief of the majority of Black Nazrawis around the world. However, Black theology that occurs in the classrooms of academia and in publications largely does not match the Black Urpeh in its commitment to the universal truth of the Bisrat. For this reason, the Gospelist paradigm affirms the biblical value of rit'at in agreement with the majority of Black Nazrawis since the beginning of the Urpeh.

## Terms

Ag'azi: Ge'ez (Ethiopic) original name for the land and people of what is now called Ethiopia; related to the Ge'ez word for "free"; this word typically appears in Ge'ez texts accompanied with the word beḥer ("region") as in, the "region of the Ag'azi."

bisrat: Geʻez (Ethiopic) word for "Good News" or "Gospel," related to various Semitic cognates from the verb "to proclaim good news"

haymanot: Geʻez (Ethiopic) word for "faith," "belief," "doctrine," "theology," related to various Semitic cognates from the verb "to believe"

Nazrawi: Geʻez (Ethiopic) word for "Christian," related to various Semitic cognates from "Nazarene"

neguś: Geʻez (Ethiopic) word for "king"

ritʻat: Geʻez (Ethiopic) word for "correctness," "rightness," "straightness," "orthodoxy"; as an adjective the word appears as ritiʻt ("orthodox")

Shajeh: Coptic (Egyptian) word for "Word" or "teaching," often used by Egyptian Nazrawis in reference to the "Word of Noute (God)," often used in reference to the "Bible"

Tilli: Old Nubian term for "God," from the name of an ancient Meroitic goddess that was used by Nubian Nazrawis to refer translate *theos* and *elohim*

Urpeh: Coptic (Egyptian) word for "temple," also used by early Egyptian Nazrawis to refer to a "church"; lit: "to do/make heaven"

# A Sankofa of the Trinity: African Patristics and Ancient Trinitarianism Informing the Praxis of the Black Church

Brooke D. Giles

## Introduction

In the African patriarchs of the church, we find an active imagination, enacting clairvoyant visions of God's nature. Their words bring a wholistic understanding of the Trinity alive with conviction and a potency which shaped their orthopraxy and colored their sociology. The compartmentalized God, seen largely in the person of Christ— the Son—is theologized in African-American contexts and western spaces and worshipped across much of the African diaspora. Yet, encountering the words of patriarchs, such as Tertullian, Origen, Athanasius, St. Yared and Shenoute, her people will envision the mystery of God with a language etched in stone by the church fathers, yet generative in imagination. This paper will survey African Patristic Trinitarianism and illuminate a deeply ingrained orthodoxy and orthopraxis. Following a cyclical model of theology, our journey will synthesize the ancient writings and models with the present condition, needs and practices of the black church and her people. In this Sankofa of trinitarian theology, I intend to first highlight the miscues in Western Trinitarianism. Then I will demonstrate a necessity for Black Nazrawis to develop what is often an anemic understanding of our Triune God and finally use this theology to galvanize a system of practices that are decentered and re-centered in the heart of the Trinity: equality, justice and love. What this paper does not seek to do is dismantle Western contributions to trinitarian theology nor reconstruct an African or African-American theology. Rather in reflecting the triune God, this study seeks to unite (or re-unite) the African-American church with its ancient theological roots as a means of finding home (Father), truth (Son) and direction for forward movement (Holy Spirit) through an embodied Trinitarianism.

## Western Trinitarianism

The polemics of African patristics were fueled with an urgency toward right theology and right practice. We often take for granted that the establishment and unfolding of this theology has been done for us and fail to engage our own divine imaginations of the mystery of the Trinity. Similar theological work is being done in the context of developing African Trinitarianism. Notable here, among many others,[136] is the work of James Henry Owino Kombo in expressing the Trinity in "ntu" metaphysics. His African contextualization of the Triune God "demands that 'Christianized Nyasaye' (Luo: God), is expressed 'Nyasaye Wuro' (God the Father), 'Nyasaye Wuowi' (God the Son) and 'Nyasaye Roho Maler' (God the Holy Spirit)."[137]

Anthropocentric theologizing is threaded throughout Western thought, as described in the following theological developments on the Trinity. This sweeping critique does not negate the contributions of these theological models but instead highlights the nuances of language

---

[136] Ibrahim S. Bitrus, *Community and Trinity in Africa* (London: Routledge, 2017), 109-123. Here Bitrus examines the works of African theologians Okechukwu Ogbonnaya, James Henry Owino Kombo, and Agbonkhianmeghe E. Orobator.

[137] James Henry Owino Kombo, *The Doctrine of God in African Christian Thought: The Holy Trinity, Theological Hermeneutics and the African Intellectual Culture* (Boston, MA: Brill, 2007), 260.

and movement that promote anthropocentricism, oppressive models of power or division within the Trinity. Models like the psychological doctrine of the Trinity, postulate from a human model of love, and then reapplies it to God, fallibly applying the *finite* to the *infinite*.[138] Similarly, Barth literally objectifies and diminishes the mystery of the Trinity within the constructs of human reality, by asserting that God, "in His Word comes as an object to man."[139] The eternal unity and impassability of the Trinity is disrupted in Moltmann's description of the cross as a moment "of deep division in God himself" where God "contradicts" himself.[140] Thomas Aquinas's two treatises *On the One God* and *On the Trinity* subordinates the doctrine of the Trinity while, in a sense, discarding the immanence of the Triune God.[141]

An additional misstep in western Trinitarianism occurs in the reduction of Trinitarian theology to a pragmatic tool for domination and oppression. Eugene Webb describes this shift in Trinitarian theology within the West. The 8th century Carolingian Filioque clause—the idea that the Son generated the Holy Spirit's very existence from within himself—served the Western Roman milieu of power by elevating Christ to "the status of a superhuman, supremely powerful individual whose authority could then be represented on earth in the person of the monarch at the head of the earthly hierarchy."[142] Trinitarian symbolism emerged in the West as a theological "interpretation that could not only countenance but also legitimate the violence of the inquisition (The Occitan subsequent inquisitions).[143] These thrusts for

---

[138] Veli-Matti Kärkkäinen, *The Trinity: Global Perspectives*, (Louisville, KY: Westminster John Knox Press, 2007), 92.

[139] Karl Barth, *Church Dogmatics The Doctrine of God, Volume 2, Part 1 : The Knowledge of God; The Reality of God*, ed. Thomas F. Torrance and Geoffrey William Bromiley, (London: T&T Clark, 2004), 10.

[140] Kärkkäinen, *The Trinity*, 104.

[141] Karl Rahner, The Trinity, (London: Continuum, 2001), 15.

[142] Eugene Webb, *In Search of the Triune God : The Christian Paths of East and West* (Columbia, Missouri: University of Missouri Press, 2014), 181.

[143] Webb, *In Search of the Triune God*, 217.

power forced a symbolic Trinity that dominated social seats and sees constructed within the bed of collective narcissism. As a result, Western theological praxis was promulgated less as a spiritual activity and more as an intellectual one.[144]

Robert W. Jenson asserts that "twentieth-century theology has learned that the doctrine of the Trinity has explanatory and interpretive use for the whole of theology."[145] Yet, the Trinity *is* the whole of theology: the Alpha and Omega of our questions and answers about God and Her creation. In these approaches, however, theologizing happens from a place of ownership, suppression and pragmatism—a very Western, imperialist posture: "Harold Carter notes that African-Americans use prayer, song, and music, inter-changing the three persons of the Trinity, according to need."[146] In pragmatically dividing the three persons of the Trinity, our ecclesiological roots are dichotomized as either "a continuation of the ancient assembly of God," in "Peter's confession at Caesarea Philippi" or in the appearance of the Holy Spirit at Pentecost, though not all three.[147] We then miss and misinterpret the power of the Holy Spirit, the incarnate Word on earth, or we fail to find relevance in the First Testament Scripture.

Without a consistent Trinitarian praxis, Black theological tradition teeters toward tritheism, nearly calling on the "gods" to serve our varying conditions of need. At the polar end, we steer clear of the mystery of the Trinity, exhibiting what Karl Rahner names as "anti-trinitarian timidity."[148] This is uniquely prominent in the Black Church tradition, where our liturgical language is skewed in ambiguous phrases like, "Father God" and a liturgical and homiletical empha-

---

[144] Webb, *In Search of the Triune God,* 200.
[145] Kärkkäinen, *The Trinity,* 67.
[146] See Harold A. Carter, *The Prayer Tradition of Black People* (Valley Forge, PA: Judson Press, 1976), 50.
[147] James H. Evans, Jr., *We Have Been Believers: An African American Systematic Theology,* (Minneapolis, MN: Fortress Press, 2012), 141.
[148] Karl Rahner, *The Trinity*, 13.

sis on Jesus as Lord. The Apostolic tradition, comprising more than 40 percent of the Black Pentecostal tradition—more specifically, the Oneness movement—emphasizes that there is one God, one Spirit and one Lord—and that is Jesus.[149] The accessibility of Jesus' humanity and suffering and the motif of Savior, in light of the ongoing oppression and need for black liberation, contributes to the prioritization of the Son in our Trinitarian approach.

While I wholeheartedly affirm the soteriological truths that uphold salvation through the Son, there is an anthropocentricism that creeps into our theology when we limit our Trinitarianism to understanding God primarily as one who saves us from exile and oppression. As demonstrated in the liberation themed songs and homiletics of the African-American tradition, our theological posture bends beneath the gaze of white, Western cultural captivity. For many Black Nazrawis, this is the point of abandonment; we deny the existence of God when he doesn't save us from our temporal oppressions. This prevalence is reflected upon by William R. Jones, who asserts that "black liberation theism is incoherent and irrational."[150] He calls instead for a "humanocentric theism," belief in God with an emphasis on humanity as the main enactors of liberation.[151] Yet, if the efforts of humanity have not rescued us from the depravity of sin and the twisted nooses of injustice, how audacious it is to consider humanity worthy of our confidence. In the Trinity, we encounter a God who is Immanuel in our suffering, yet has mystery beyond the ills and pains from which we cry out. Will we chase after this mystery or bottle the Creator into a medicinal convenience?

---

[149] Frederick L. Ware, *African American Theology: An Introduction*, (Louisville, KY: Westminster, 2016), 83.
[150] Ware, *African American Theology*, 84.
[151] Ware, *African American Theology*, 84.

# African Patristic Trinitarianism

## Tertullian

We turn now to Tertullian (A.D. 145-220), who asserts that "God is one or he does not exist."[152] He contends for the correct understanding of the Triune God as "supreme being, existing in eternity, unborn, uncreated, without beginning, without end."[153] David Wilhite affirms Tertullian's distinctly African, Christian, non-imperial perspective and voice. This is especially evident in writings such as *De Pallio* and *Apologeticum*, where he claims Africa as his homeland (*patria*), and *Ad Nationes*.[154] Tertullian's ridicule of the plethora of Roman gods in *Ad Nationes* not only draws a religio-cultural distinction but provides context to his adamant insistence for a 'right understanding' of the Triune God or none at all.

Gifting to Trinitarian theology a vocabulary of expression including *trinitas, persona* and *substantia*, Tertullian develops an understanding of Father, Son and Spirit as one. While imperfect, this provides a basis from which later councils and theologians crystallized an understanding of the Trinity for the catholic church. From Tertullian we see that the Trinity is an eternal reality of who God is, versus an identity of God, only realized on the cross:

> God's eternal nature precluded change or transformation. Transformation involves the destruction of what originally existed: what is transformed ceases to be what it was and

---

[152] Tertullian, *Adversus Marcionem*, ed. Henry Bettenson and Henry Scowcroft Bettenson., *The Early Christian Fathers: A Selection from the Writings of the Fathers from St. Clement of Rome to St. Athanasius,* (Oxford: Oxford University Press, 1969), 104.

[153] Tertullian, *Adversus Marcionem*, 104.

[154] David Wilhite, *Tertullian the African: An Anthropological Reading of Tertullian's Context and Identities* (New York, NY: Walter de Gruyter, 2007), 67-70.

begins to be something else. But God does not cease to be, nor can he be other than what he is.[155]

There is no division between who one is and what one does, as Western thought tends to compartmentalize identity and function, creating a seemingly insurmountable trench between the Bisrat and the work of justice: "The Son is not other than the Father by separation from him but by difference of function, nor by division but by distinction: for the Father and the Son are not identical but distinct in degree."[156] The nuance of language is key in differentiating African patristic thought on the Trinity and typical modern Western approaches, which tends to equate distinction with division—in theology, anthropology, economics and sociology. Thus far in Tertullian, the Black Church can find its footing as "converts" who maintain their theological and cultural heritage, instead of "proselytes" who must "sacrifice national and social identities" while inheriting the "accumulated experience" of white, Western culture.[157]

His imagery is the root, shoot and the fruit; the spring, river and canal; and the sun, the ray and point of focus. These awaken the imagination to envision God who is diverse in person and expression, yet one in substance. Tertullian's trinitarianism focuses more on the procession and prioritizes the unity of the persons of the Triune God: "Thus, the Trinity derives from the Father by continuous and connected steps; and it in no way impugns the monarchy while it preserves the reality of the 'economy'."[158]

---

[155] Tertullian, *Adversus Praxean*, ed. Henry Bettenson and Henry Scowcroft Bettenson., *The Early Christian Fathers: A Selection from the Writings of the Fathers from St. Clement of Rome to St. Athanasius,* (Oxford England: Oxford University Press, 1969), 124.
[156] Tertullian, *Adversus Praxean*, 121.
[157] A.F. Walls, "Old Athens and New Jerusalem: Some Signposts for Christian Scholarship in the Early History of Mission Studies" in *International Bulletin of Missionary Research* 21.4, 146-153, (1997): 148.
[158] Tertullian, *Adversus Praxean*, 124.

The exegesis of Tertullian on Mt. 27:46 asserts that the Son crying out his forsakenness, "was the cry of flesh and soul (that is, of man), not of the Word and the Spirit (that is, not of God); and it was uttered for the very purpose of showing the impassibility of God who thus forsook his Son in delivering his humanity to death."[159] This is the miracle of Immanuel on the cross, that God is one with the suffering of humanity, yet impassible. For the Black Nazrawi, in understanding this dynamic of the Trinity we can divorce from a fallible ideation of a temporal life, free from bearing the crosses of oppression. Instead, through Tertullian's Trinitarian imagination, our liturgy, homiletics and social engagement reveals a Triune God who does not anesthetize our trauma but knows and is united with us in our suffering, as he ushers our pain into his glorious, redemptive purposes.

In light of the Black church's often "either-or" relationship with the Holy Spirit (embraced with fervency or trepidation depending on the tradition), Tertullian's reflections on the Spirit are invaluable. He writes that the Paraclete was sent "that discipline might progressively be guided, ordered, and brought to perfection by his representative, the Holy Spirit" and that the Spirit is "the guidance of discipline, the interpretation of Scripture, the reformation of the intellect, the advance towards better things."[160] Do our church bodies, likewise, model an outward progression of discipleship, theological and social advancement? If not, are we misaligned with the model set before us by the nature of our God?

## Athanasius

In line with Tertullian, Athanasius (ca. 300-373), who wrote extensively on the Holy Spirit, honored the unity of the Trinity as

---

[159] Tertullian, *Adversus Praxean*, 124-125.
[160] Tertullian, *De Virginibus Velandis*, ed. Henry Bettenson and Henry Scowcroft Bettenson., *The Early Christian Fathers: A Selection from the Writings of the Fathers from St. Clement of Rome to St. Athanasius,* (Oxford: Oxford University Press, 1969), 130.

"indivisible and of one nature."[161] He declares the "ever perfect" triunity of God: "Never was the substance of the Father incomplete, so that what belonged to it should be added afterwards."[162] Athanasius' use of imagery wonderfully describes the Father as the fountain, the Son as the river and invites the diversity of humanity to drink of the one Spirit.[163] With consistent repetition and in step with other African patristic writers, he uses attributive qualifiers like "Holy", "of God", "of the Father", and "My" from First Testament texts to refute the Tropicist (and Arian) exegesis of Amos 4:13 which designates the Holy Spirit as a creature.[164]

Athanasius' use of the Old Testament broadens beyond the function of addressing heretics to harmoniously annotate the eternal existence of the Trinity active in the experiences of ancient Israel. He writes, "they drank of a spiritual rock that followed them, and the rock was Christ."[165] Bringing in Peter's confession at Caesarea Philippi, the same rock that followed God's chosen people is the life-giving rock of Christ—one of three in the Trinity—on which the impregnable church is built. Do we imagine our exegesis as an embodiment of the Trinity, oscillating harmoniously between Testaments of the Shajeh (Coptic: Word)?

Further, the ecclesiological implications of Athanasius and his use of 1 Cor. 10 and 12 are resounding, especially for our Western, racialized church and the spores of divisiveness that develop from a multiplicity of sources. He asserts that when the Apostle writes: "Now there are varieties of gifts, but the same Spirit; and there are varieties of service, but the same Lord; and there are varieties of activities,

---

[161] Athanasius, *To Serapion On The Holy Spirit,* in *The Christian Theology Reader*, ed. Alister E. McGrath, (New York, NY: John Wiley & Sons, 2016), 25.

[162] Athanasius, *Select treatises of St. Athanasius in controversy with the Arians*, ed. John Henry Newman, (London: Longmans, Green, and Co., 1900), 350.

[163] Athanasius, *To Serapion On The Holy Spirit*, 27-28.

[164] Athanasius, *To Serapion On The Holy Spirit*, 4-13.

[165] Athanasius, *To Serapion On The Holy Spirit*, 28.

but it is the same God who empowers them all in everyone,"[166] that Paul "finds the source of all things in one God, the Father."[167] As Black Nazrawis, our praxis of worship, civic engagement, social transformation and evangelism must be a Trinitarian praxis, a synchronous forward movement in step with the "same Spirit, same Lord and same God?"

That the unity of our ecclesial membership is held within the unity of the Trinity further validates the necessity for our theology to be centered in the Trinity. Likewise, our apologetics must address, with the same fervor as the African patriarchs, the heretical doctrines that misconstrue the image of our Triune God. Our spiritual health and the *rit'at* of our praxes depend on it. However, in my experience with modern Black churches, we adopt a catch-all (or catch-none) approach to various Trinitarian doctrines and miss opportunities to offer a gracious invitation into right belief—a belief that must, essentially begin with the Trinity. Athanasius' model, in *Ad Serapion* and *Contra Arianos*, admonishes the heretics to save the heresy for the Greeks, the Caesareans and men of Scythopolis. Yet, he doesn't leave them wanting in a muddle of intelligibility regarding the mystery of the Trinity, as he plainly paints a portrait of the tripartite theophany:

> The Father does all things through the Word in the Holy Spirit; and thus, the unity of the Holy Trinity is preserved; and thus, there is preached in the Church one God [...] He is "over all" as Father, as an origin or a fountain; he is "through all", through the Word; and he is "in all", in the Holy Spirit. It is a Trinity, not only in name and in a form of words, but in truth and in actuality (reality).[168]

---

[166] 1 Cor. 12:4-6, All scriptural references are taken from the English Standard Version (ESV), unless otherwise noted.
[167] Athanasius, *To Serapion On The Holy Spirit*, 29.
[168] Athanasius, *To Serapion On The Holy Spirit,* 167.

The Trinity is eternal, active and moves in a choreography of united co-ordination "within the holy Triad."[169] To question the unity of our Triune God is to subjugate the diversities of God to a sense of foreignness or alienation, likened by Athanasius to futile attempts to divide "the radiance from the light, or wisdom from the wise."[170] The impossibility of these attempts reflects "the audacity of madmen to make such [divisive] inquiries concerning God." [171] I add, the audacious attempts to divide the Bisrat from the work of justice and to divide God's people are the putrid fruits of this madness.

## Origen

Origen's Trinitarian theology is systematically organized around Apostolic teaching as revealed through the Holy Scripture, which in itself is fruit of the economy of the Trinity. With clarity, Origen structures his primary locus on the Triune God:

> First, That there is one God, who created and arranged all things, and who, when nothing existed, called all things into being…Secondly, that Jesus Christ Himself, who came (into the world), was born of the Father before all creatures…Then, Thirdly, the apostles related that the Holy Spirit was associated in honor and dignity with the Father and the Son…and that this Spirit inspired each one of the saints, whether prophets or apostles.[172]

Necessarily refuting the assertion that God is a body, a heresy purported by Monarchianists, Origen's Trinitarian theology thus

---

[169] Athanasius, *To Serapion On The Holy Spirit*, 29.
[170] Athanasius, *To Serapion On The Holy Spirit*, 30.
[171] Athanasius, *To Serapion On The Holy Spirit*, 30.
[172] Origen, *De Principiis* in *The Ante-Nicene Fathers: Translations of the Writings of the Fathers Down to A.d. 325, Vol. 4,* ed. Phillip Schaff, Alexander Roberts, James Donaldson, et al, (Grand Rapids, MI: Eerdmans, 1885), 423-424.

centers itself on the "absolute transcendence and incorporeality of the divine"[173] and the fullness of the Son's humanity is highlighted: "In our prayers we must take care both to preserve the duality and to bring in the unity."[174] He is heavy-handed in his use of Scripture and thoroughly employs the Spirit-breathed word to fuse the movement of our eternal Father, Son and Spirit in an extra-temporal flow between the First and New Testaments. The space of this occasion does not provide room to squeeze in an adequate survey of Origen's Trinitarianism. His contributions especially honor the person of the Holy Spirit "who, by the providence of God through the Word who was 'in the beginning with God' (Jn. 1:1), enlightened the servants of the truth."[175] Origen writes: "[The Holy Spirit's] purpose is for us to 'become partaker of all the doctrines of the Spirit's counsel;' by searching out and devoting [ourselves] to the 'deep things' (1 Cor. 2:10) revealed in the spiritual meaning of the words."[176]

The mystery of the Trinity then, is understood through the mystery of the Trinity. This good news is nestled even deeper in the beautiful imagery Origen offers. Through the obscure Psalm 68:13, he further pursues for his audience an imbibing of the inspired Word in his *Homily 27 on Luke 3.18–22*:

> For, if we rest "between the plots" of the Old and New Testaments, "silver wings of a dove" will be given to us, that is, the words of God, and the pinions of its tail, radiant with the gleam of gold, so that our senses might be filled with perceptions of the Holy Spirit—that is, our speech and our mind filled by his coming, and we would neither speak nor understand anything

---

[173] Bilal Baş, "Orthodoxy of Origen of Alexandria's Trinitarian Doctrine: Is His Theology Arian or Nicene?" *Marmara Üniversitesi İlahiyat Fakültesi Dergisi* 37.2, 93-110 (2009): 101.
[174] Origen, *Dialogue with Heraclites*, in *Documents*, in *Early Christian Thought*, ed. Maurice Wiles and Mark Santer, 22-42, (Cambridge: Cambridge University Press, 1975), 25.
[175] Origen, *De Principiis*, 445.
[176] Origen, *De Principiis*, 445.

besides what he suggests. That way, all sanctification, both in our hearts and in our words and deeds, might come from the Holy Spirit in Christ Jesus, to whom is glory and power for ages of ages. Amen.[177]

Even in the realm of theological scholarship, how blessed it is for the black theologian to find herself in the trenches of colonized thought, now "filled with perceptions of the Holy Spirt" given by the "silver wings" of God's word and sanctified to speak and understand only what is suggested from the Spirit in Christ Jesus. Thus, studies of the Shajeh, in its entirety, and rich theological scholarship cannot be an aside to the preached moment and other liturgical praxes. The implications here are vast, however, to rest momentarily in this inspiration from the Trinitarian thought of Origen, it is necessary and a fitting transition to the theology of Coptic and Ethiopic Christianity.

## Shenoute

The Egyptian monastic leader, Shenoute the Great, (ca. 347–465) invoked the Trinity throughout his discourses, shaping a particularly Coptic orthodox tradition. His discourse arises from the heresy of "the great enemy of humanity," Arius.[178] Like Athanasius, he expounds on the eternality of the Trinity. Shenoute honors the single essence of Father, Son and Spirit, describing the Son as "God from God."[179] Still the humanity of the Son is complete: "He hungered. He thirsted. He wept. He grieved at the hardheartedness of those who were unbelievers. And finally, he died for us."[180] In Shenoute's Trinitarianism, humanity

---

[177] Origen, *Homily 27 on Luke 3:18-22,* in *Homilies on Luke,* ed. Joseph T. Lienhard, (Washington, DC: Catholic University of America Press, 1996), 114.

[178] Shenoute, *I Am Amazed,* ed. David Brakke and Andrew Crislip, in *Selected Discourses of Shenoute the Great: Community, Theology, and Social Conflict in Late Antique Egypt* (Cambridge: Cambridge University Press, 2015), 58.

[179] Shenoute, *I Am Amazed,* 74.

[180] Shenoute, *I Am Amazed,* 74.

meets the divine in worship, orthodoxy and orthopraxis. Shenoute warns against those who, with weakened Christology, hesitate to pray in the name of Jesus:

> Our prayers, "In the name of Jesus" are prayers to the Triune God. You are blessed, O God, you and your blessed Son, whose names—yours and his—become one in the mouth of whoever opposes those who speak this new impiety.[181]

Mindful of the propensity to suppress the Trinity into the person of Yeshua, He repeats throughout his sermons: "In calling the name of the Son, we call the holy Trinity."[182] He also uses the calls to baptize using both the Triune names of God (Mt. 28:19) and the name of Jesus (Gal. 3:27, Rom. 6:3). This clarification is essential, because an incomplete, partial imbibing of trinitarian theology means an incomplete praxis of honoring the Trinity.

Shenoute does not, however, assume that a Trinitarian praxis is confined to the liturgy. His deliberateness in embracing a holistic doctrine of the Trinity is reflected in his work with the white monastery and advocating for the poor and marginalized of his society: "For if we do not fear the cries of those who groan, neither will we fear the judgment of the Son of God."[183]

The rhythm and repetition of his sermon is reminiscent of my days sitting in the pews of North Main Missionary Baptist Church. I can imagine the timbre of his voice, a reverb of Trinitarian thought:

> Seek the perfection of these words and you will find them in your mouth and the mouths of your children. As you celebrate

---

[181] Shenoute, *I Am Amazed*, 79.

[182] Shenoute, *I Am Amazed*, 81.

[183] Shenoute, *As I Began To Preach,* ed. David Brakke and Andrew Crislip, *Selected Discourses of Shenoute the Great: Community, Theology, and Social Conflict in Late Antique Egypt* (Cambridge: Cambridge University Press, 2015), 190.

and rejoice, "Jesus," and as you sorrow and grieve, "Jesus." As boys and girls laugh, "Jesus." They who ford a body of water, "Jesus." They who flee in the face of barbarians, "Jesus." They who see wild beasts and a terrifying event, "Jesus." They who are in pains and illnesses, "Jesus." They who are taken captive, "Jesus." They whose justice is perverted and are treated violently, "Jesus." In every circumstance it is the name of Jesus that is in their mouths and is their salvation and also their life with his Father.[184]

## St. Yared, Walatta Petros and Ethiopian Trinitarianism

The church in Ethiopia is rich with its own unique orthodoxy and an ecclesiastical heritage that is etched into its core. The fourth century Ezana Stelae, an inscription of the early Aksumite King Ezana, evidences Trinitarian theology that pre-dates the Council of Chalcedon by approximately 100 years.[185] It states: "By faith in God and by the power of the Father and Son and Holy Spirit, to the one who saved the kingdom."[186] King Ezana's words call upon the Trinity as his "help" in defeating the Noba people. The Ezana Stelae bears witness to the abundance of Trinitarian thought flowing beyond the church through Aksum's headship and imperial structures.

Our exploration of Trinitarian thought in the Ethiopian context moves now to St. Yared, who continues the paradigm of rich contextualization and continues the lineage of African patristic trinitarianism. The Degwa, a distinctly Ethiopian form of canticles and original

---

[184] Shenoute, *I Am Amazed*, 81.

[185] Stephanie L. Black, "In the Power of God Christ: Greek Inscriptional Evidence for the Anti-Arian Theology of Ethiopia's First Christian King," in *Bulletin of the School of Oriental and African Studies, University of London* 71.1, 93-110 (2008):110.

[186] Black, "In the Power of God Christ," 102.

literary text was developed by St. Yared and a part of the liturgy of the Tawahedo church. The later development of liturgy and canticles are the weft of the Ethiopian Church's theological tapestry and Trinitarianism: "They conveyed Christian song and chant earlier and closer to the heart of Sub-Saharan Africa than any other written tradition."[187] Yared's extensive collection of poetry and hymns arises from his ascension experience, depicted in *the Acts of Yared:* "when God understood his heart, he sent three birds [representing the Father, Son and Holy Spirit] to him from the Garden of Paradise, in the likeness of the Trinity."[188] Taking three distinct forms, this liturgical chant is birthed from a cognizant attachment to the persons of the Triune God: "*Ge'ez* with the almighty Father (eliciting awe), *'ezl* with the anguish of the Son (empathic with suffering), *araray* with the fulfilling work of the Holy Spirit."[189] They form a unity of song, just as the triune teaching points to the oneness of God the Father, Son, and Spirit.

St. Yared's poetry and psalmody follow "Alexandrian [and Ephremaic] exegetical tradition, including Origen, as it approaches the Old and New Testaments as a single book corresponding to the one Logos."[190] As we have seen this commonality among African patristics, the unity of the Trinity is carried even into exegetical methods. St. Yared employs this same unity in gender, referencing the Son as both "mother" and "father," a signifier of the ancient roots of his writings.[191]

> Your cross, O Lord, resurrects the dead, helps those who are in the abyss, is calmness for the sea, a harbor for the ships,

---

[187] Peter Jeffrey, *The Songs of Africa: The Ethiopian Canticles,* ed., Thomas C. Oden and Curt Niccum, (New Haven, CT: ICCS Press, 2017), 2.
[188] Ralph Lee, "Symbolic Interpretations in Ethiopic and Ephremaic Literature," Ph.D. diss. (University of London, 2011), 34.
[189] Jeffrey, *The Songs of Africa,* 5.
[190] Lee, *Symbolic Interpretations,* 39-40.
[191] Jeffrey, *The Songs of Africa,* 17.

Christ is father and mother for the whole world. His apostles he circuited, the feet of his disciples he washed, He became father and mother for them and taught them wisdom.[192]

That he recognizes that totality with which the Triune God has manifested throughout creation should inform black church praxis and tradition that often engages in its own marginalizing praxes when dissenting against gender and sexuality issues. The homily of St. Yared instructs us that unity of Father, Son and Holy Spirit precedes and supersedes the divisiveness and marginalization of women through patriarchal inventions.

From the 5th century epiclesis, *The Testament of Our Lord* to the *Kedasse of the Apostles*, to the *Kebra Negast*, and many more Ethiopic texts, the Trinity is referenced and prominent within this body of literature. Important to mention are the hagiographies of two African women, Krəstos Śämra and, most substantially, Walatta Petros, which flourish with symbols and references to the Triune God. In *The Life and Struggles of Our Mother Walatta Petros,* Galäwdewos depicts the mother's spiritual resilience using a lyric from a St. Yared hymn: "Having taken three names, I lean on a staff. Even if I fall, I stand up again."[193] Here, the three names—the Trinity is connected to a reference to Micah. This continues the practice of patristic writing to exegete from both Testaments as one spiritually integrated text. Even the many names within the biography of Walatta Petros, such as *Za Selasse* ("The One from the Trinity"), *Hiruta Salasse* ("The Benevolence of the Trinity"), *Walatta Sellasse* ("Daughter of the Trinity"), signify the elevation of Trinitarian thought within ancient Ethiopian

---

[192] Jeffrey, *The Songs of Africa*, 349-350.
[193] Galäwdewos, *The Life and Struggles of Our Mother Walatta Petros: A Seventeenth-Century African Biography of an Ethiopian Woman,* ed. Wendy Laura Belcher and Michael Kleiner, (Princeton, NJ: Princeton University Press, 2015), 160.

Christianity. It is a *rit'at* that is preserved and uniquely characteristic of Ethiopia to this day.[194]

Finally, in the hagiographic poem *Hail Walatta*, her laudable faith and character are elevated with esteem:

> Hail to you, Walatta Petros, a mirror! You reveal the Trinity
> in its holiness to everyone, high and low:
> now the faithful sit safe on dry ground.[195]

This is her reflection of the diversity of character and spirituality of the Father, Son and Spirit that deem her worthy to be hailed before men. It is unlike our reduction of the character of God to terms like, "Christ-like" and "Godly." Again, we witness a cognizant acknowledgement of the fullness of God in the most fundamental and most profound ways in ancient African texts.

## Conclusion

We return now, asking what does the orthopraxis of the Black church have to do with the Trinity? Our work of being the people of Tilli—Father, Son and Spirit—in the world is undergirded with explicit instruction from the teachings of African patristic Trinitarianism and rooted in a harmonious fusion of both testaments as one Word. The black theologian must assert his divinely gifted, unique contexts and cultural perspectives, just as our predecessors pushed against the Trinitarian missteps of the colonizing, dominant culture. Our ministerial work must consider how our homiletical and liturgical traditions serve doxological, ecclesial and didactic praxes of the Trinity. In embracing an ever-growing understanding of the fullness of our Triune God, we fuse this with our identity as the *imago dei*. We must ask of ourselves: "Are we a reflection of this flourishing

---

[194] Galäwdewos, *Walatta Petros*, 113, 182, 187.
[195] Galäwdewos, *Walatta Petros*, 381.

movement of unity within diversity in the world in the way we, the black church, enact economic and educational equality, social and legal justice and through creative practices rooted in the love of our Triune God?" We must, through our homilies, our song, our scriptural, cultural and relational exegesis, engage in a Sankofa of the Trinity. This is the truth, our dwelling place, the home to which we must thoughtfully return. Our going back is our way forward.

In following the tradition of St. Yared, I offer this:

## A Poem On the Trinity For Today

In the Trinity we listen and know
Humanity and movement of spirit embodied
In reverence
And in rest

What is imagined when we speak your name Elohim
In need, we cry Abba, Father
Inspired, we honor Holy Spirit
In worship we are brought to the cross

Yet you Tilli are the three
One God, diverse in unity
Will we be silent among those
Who only name you as the Son
Will we struggle with vain mumblings
To encapsulate your glory in our human understanding
Or will we speak of you as the three and one
And surrender to what is beyond word
Only existing in thought
And remembering you beyond thought
Seeing visions of you in our dreams

And when our dreams fail
The silver wings and gold-dipped pinions of your truth
Carry us from eternity to eternity
Immanuel, we Hope for you
beyond what our imaginations can contain
Until we can behold
The awe, Ge'ez
The sorrow, 'ezl
The fulfillment of your perfection, araray

And until then
We will speak of you the everlasting Spring, remembering you in the river's flow
Tasting of your goodness, we drink as one
We will sing of you as we behold the Son, its rays are your warmth,
Its illuminating focus comforts us beholding your glory with the Father and Spirit
Sweet, Holy Spirit
We will surrender to you
Listening to your whispers in the dark of oppression
Watching your fresh wind dance through the joy of creation
An inaudible conversation
Spirit hovering
Word bringing forth life
becoming flesh
Knowing us
Loving Us
Moving Us
The whole of you is YHWH
wind of the Paraclete
Immanuel
We hope for you in the hunger of empty bellies

We seek the fullness of who you are in the questioning eyes of oppressed bodies
We find the humanity of your son in our brokenness
Nyasaye Wuro
Nyasaye Wuowi
Nyasaye Roho Maler

We draw near to the one
Our divisiveness of thought melts before your oneness
Your union disrupts the discord
And draws your body, ever closer
United in flesh to you
Distinctly one
All the same
Wholly yours
Until forever
Rest in me
Us three
How will we pray.
In Yeshua, we speak the Trinity
As you formed us from the dust.
Holy. Holy. Holy.
In the wilderness.
Your Word walked among us.
Holy. Holy. Holy.
In the anguish of the cross.
Holy. Holy. Holy.
You rose with all power.
Your Spirit stirs us.
Holy. Holy. Holy.
Our fathers wrote of you.
Holy. Holy. Holy.

In chains.
A mass of bodies behind cold steel bars.
Holy. Holy. Holy.
As we feed your people
And offer ourselves in Word and protest.
Holy. Holy. Holy.
In our imaginings.
In song.
We say Amen to the three.

# Black Lives Matter: Inside the Womb and Out

## Aaron Turner

"Black lives matter!" rings out at protests across the country.[196] The mantra has become an effective rhetorical tool to protest suspected police brutality against black Americans. While thoughtful Christians should have many places where they disagree with the Black Lives Matter organization,[197] the simple statement "black lives matter" should be non-controversial for Christians since it is theologically certain. God's Word tells us that "black lives matter" when it reveals to us that all human beings are made in the image/likeness of God (see Gen. 1:26-27, 9:6, Jas. 3:9). If a person or group is made in the image of God, their lives matter--they matter to God, and therefore ought to matter to everyone else! Again, the assertion that "black lives matter" should be non-controversial. However, in a country that has historically despised black skin and in certain areas of our national life

---

[196] Larry Buchanon argues that the Black Lives Matter Movement could be the largest movement in American history. Larry Buchanan, "Black Lives Matter May Be the Largest Movement in U.S. History," *The New York Times,* July 3, 2020, https://www.nytimes.com/interactive/2020/07/03/us/george-floyd-protests-crowd-size.html.

[197] Albert Mohler does a good job highlighting some of the areas of concern with the Black Lives Matter organization: Albert Mohler, "The Briefing: Thursday, June 18th, 2020", *Albert Mohler,* June 18th, 2020, https://albertmohler.com/2020/06/18/briefing-6-18-20.

still treats black people unequally,[198] it does make sense to explicitly affirm that "black lives matter."

## Where Black Lives Don't Matter

The Black Lives Matter movement has largely focused the nation's attention on the killing of black people by police. While it is good for our culture to wrestle with the question "are black lives really being valued when it comes to the use of deadly force by police against black citizens," a far greater danger against black lives is going unnoticed and often unprotested by the black community. I am speaking of the danger posed to black lives via abortion. When all is said and done, I fear that my community, the black community, may end up being guilty of "straining out a gnat and swallowing a camel!"[199] If black lives are to truly matter in this country, they must matter where they are most at risk. The most dangerous place to be black in America is not in a car pulled over by a police officer; nor is it in the "hood" of some major American city. The most dangerous place to be black in America is inside a mother's womb. Until black lives matter in the womb, they don't truly matter in America.

---

[198] Here are three examples: 1) Evidence seems to indicate that black male offenders seem to get longer sentences than similarly situated white male offenders, see "Demographic Differences In Sentencing," United States Sentencing Commission, November 14th, 2017, https://www.ussc.gov/research/research-reports/demographic-differences-sentencing 2) Evidence seems to indicate that black Americans, when compared with white Americans, are discriminated against in how often their cars are searched during traffic stops, see "Findings", *The Stanford Open Policing Project*, 2020, https://openpolicing.stanford.edu/findings/ and Michelle Alexander, *The New Jim Crow: Mass Incarceration in the Age of Colorblindness* (New York: The New Press, 2012), 133-134; 3) Evidence seems to indicate that individuals are far more likely to get the death penalty if they kill a white person versus if they kill a black person, and that even though many people who are sentenced to death never are actually executed, the execution is more likely to be carried out if the individual's victim was white, as opposed to black, see Adam Liptak, "A Vast Racial Gap in Death Penalty Cases, New Study Finds," *The New York Times*, August 3, 2020, https://www.nytimes.com/2020/08/03/us/racial- gap-death-penalty.html.

[199] Mt. 23:24. Unless otherwise noted, all biblical citations are taken from the English Standard Version (ESV).

## The Facts of the Matter

It would be hard to exaggerate the extent to which abortion is decimating the black population in America. Approximately 14% of women in the U.S. are black but according to the CDC, based off the data they had from 32 states, 38% of the nation's abortions are performed on black women.[200] For comparison purposes, "non-Hispanic white women make up 60% of the population but account for only 35-39% of all abortions."[201] Therefore, while white women greatly outnumber black women in our country, both groups account for approximately the same total number of abortions. This means that black babies are killed at a much greater rate than white babies. One horrifying example of the destruction wrought by abortion on the black community is the effect on the black population in New York City. In 2013, black women were the recipients of 42% of New York City's abortions, and tragically more black babies were aborted that year in New York City than were born.[202] Staying with New York City but broadening out beyond the year 2013, Jason Riley reported: "According to a city Health Department report released in May, between 2012 and 2016 black mothers terminated 136,426 pregnancies and gave birth to 118,127

---

[200] "Women of Color in the United States: Quick Take", *Catalyst*, March 19, 2020. https://www.catalyst.org/research/women-of-color-in-the-united-states/.; Kimberly Leonard, "CDC: Two Percent Fewer Women Getting Abortions", *Washington Examiner*, November 27, 2019, https://www.washingtonexaminer.com/policy/healthcare/cdc-two-percent-fewer-women-getting-abortions. In this article whenever I speak of abortion, and as far as I can tell whenever I use information from other sources about abortions, the reference is to "surgical abortions", and is not addressing the widespread and tragic phenomena of "medical abortions". One can only imagine how much worse the picture might be if our discussion included "medical abortions".

[201] "Abortion and Race: For decades, abortion has disproportionately eliminated minority babies", Abort 73.com, last modified July 9, 2020, https://abort73.com/abortion/abortion_and_race/.

[202] Lauren Caruba, "Cynthia Meyer Says More Black Babies are Aborted in New York City than Born". *Politifact*, , last modified December 1st 2015, https://www.politifact.com/factchecks/2015/nov/25/cynthia-meyer/cynthia-meyer-says-more-black-babies-are-aborted-n/.

babies. By contrast, births far surpassed abortions among whites, Asians and Hispanics."[203] Now, if you were trying to do the math quickly, that means that 18,299 more black babies were aborted in New York between the years 2012-2016 than were born. To put the matter succinctly: Abortion is the #1 cause of death among black Americans today, by far.[204] In fact, if we consider three of the top leading causes of death for black Americans in 2015, namely heart disease, diabetes mellitus, and homicide, we find that more black babies die from abortion than from all three of those leading causes combined. And not only a little bit more, but at least twice over, and likely three times over.[205]

These statistics should shock us, better yet they should horrify us, for *all* "black lives matter". These are not just statistics. They are a holocaust of precious brown and black babies, made in the

---

[203] Jason L. Riley, "Let's Talk About The Black Abortion Rate", *The Wall Street Journal*, July 10th, 2018, https://www.wsj.com/articles/lets-talk-about-the-black-abortion-rate-1531263697.

[204] W. Gardner Selby, "Jason Isaac Makes Mostly False Claim that Abortion is the Leading Killer of Black Americans", *Politifact: The Poynter Institute*, March 2nd, 2018, https://www.politifact.com/factchecks/2018/mar/02/jason-isaac/jason-isaac-makes-mostly-false-claim-abortion-lead/. The irony of this article is that though it seeks to debunk Jason Issac's assertion that abortion is the leading cause of death for black Americans, it actually proves that he is right. The article simply labels Isaac's claim as "mostly false" because the CDC happens to not consider abortion as a cause of death. The problem here, however, is not with Isaac's assertion but with the CDC's not labeling abortion as a real cause of death.

[205] My reasoning is as follows: 1.) First, a table posted on the CDC website (likely created by another government agency) estimated that 98,291 black people died from the three mentioned causes in 2015; 2.) The Guttmacher Institute estimated that there were 862,000 abortions in 2017; 3.) If 38% (the estimate referenced earlier in my article from the CDC, see above) of these 862,000 abortions in 2017 were black babies then a total of 327,560 black babies were aborted in 2017, which is more than three times the amount of black people who died in 2015 from the aforementioned three leading causes of death for black people. In support of #1 for this footnote see: "Table 19: Leading causes of death and numbers of deaths, by sex, race, and Hispanic origin: United States, 1980 and 2015", page 1, 2016. https://www.cdc.gov/nchs/data/hus/2016/019.pdf. In support of #1 for this footnote see: The Associated Press, "Number of Abortions in U.S. Drops to Lowest Since They Became Legal Nationwide, Report Finds", NBC News, Sept 1, 2019, https://www.nbcnews.com/news/us-news/number-abortions-u-s-drops-lowest-they-became-legal-nationwide-n1055726.

image of God, who have been snuffed out as if they were merely biological matter. They are not merely matter—they matter! Not even the Ku Klux Klan of the early to mid-1900's could have likely dreamed up a more diabolical system and practice to bring about the decimation and devaluation of the black community as has the present day system and practice of abortion. The American abortion enterprise is an intolerable injustice, for the unborn of all ethnicities, but disproportionately so, as we have seen, for black unborn babies. The significant and evil effect of this system on black babies demands a response from anyone who truly believes that "black lives matter".

## Since Black Lives Really Do Matter

How should the church of Jesus Christ respond to such a crisis in the black community, given that black lives do most definitely matter? The first thing that we ought to do is pray often against the abortion holocaust that is killing off the weakest and most vulnerable among us, disproportionately so in the black community. Christians should not doubt the importance of prayer, for we recognize that "we do not wrestle against flesh and blood, but against the rulers, against the authorities, against the cosmic powers over this present darkness, against the spiritual forces of evil in the heavenly places."[206] Prayer is a more important weapon in this battle than any of us imagine.

After we pray, or better yet even while we are praying, there are some practical things that those of us who make up the black Christian community can do to help turn back the tide on this crisis. First, black churches need to speak up on this issue. From my own personal experience in the black church and from my conversations with fellow black clergy, the black church seems to be largely

---

[206] Eph. 6:12.

silent on the abortion crisis taking place in our community.[207] This may be because pastors are not aware of how serious the crisis is. It may be that they fear sounding too politically conservative. It may even be that they desire to address root systemic issues. But, whatever the hindrances may be, black churches need to speak up on this issue out of faithfulness to God and love for their unborn neighbor and kin.

Another thing that black Christians and churches can do to help with this crisis, is to come alongside black women—and especially black single mothers—assuring them that if they decide to keep their baby, the Body of Christ will be there to support them all along the way. Though we have looked at the issue of abortion through a racial lens up to this point, it is helpful also to view it as well from an economic lens. As of 2016 close to "half of abortion patients in the United States are poor and another 26% are low income."[208] This means that many of our black women who are having abortions are doing so because they fear not being able to adequately provide for themselves and their families should they go through with their pregnancy. Thus, black churches must come alongside black women assuring them that they will be there to support them over the long term should they carry their baby to term. Given the current crisis, it would be advisable for black churches to set aside significant portions of their budget to assist black mothers in this way. We should anticipate that Satan and the world will frequently point to poverty and the uncertainty of a good support network as reasons to

---

[207] Though, of course, there are likely plenty of notable exceptions such as the largely African-American Church of God in Christ (COGIC) denomination which, in 2019, formally expressed their opposition to elective abortions in their "Resolution on The Sanctity of life" (see Alexandra Desanctis, "The Pro-Life Movement You've Never Heard Of", *National Review*, March 19, 2020, https://www.nationalreview.com/magazine/2020/04/06/the-pro-life-movement-youve-never-heard-of/.

[208] "Abortion Patients are Disproportionately Poor and Low Income", Guttmacher Institute, May 9th, 2016, https://www.guttmacher.org/infographic/2016/abortion-patients-are-disproportionately-poor-and-low-income.

justify a black mother killing her unborn child. By supporting black mothers, this tactic can be defanged.

Somewhat along these lines, it would be powerful to see a movement of black Christians, heartbroken over this crisis, eager to adopt black children from moms who, out of great courage, carried their child to term, even though they concluded that they could not adequately care for their child given life's circumstances. Even though not all black Christians or black families can afford to adopt, black pastors should encourage those who can to consider doing so, out of their love for Christ and community.

Another very practical thing that the black church can do in its teaching ministry is to often lift high the Bible's teaching on sexual intimacy being a gift exclusively for the marriage bed. As of 2018, 69% of black children were born out of wedlock.[209] Having children outside of wedlock contributes to the financial poverty of black families, which in turn contributes to the temptation for black women to pursue an abortion. Anything black churches can do to discourage sex outside of wedlock, and to encourage the importance of the consistent presence of a father once a child is born is helpful in the pursuit of reducing the black abortion rate. Regarding the latter, the consistent presence of a father not only increases the financial wealth of the black family, but also social support for black mothers.

Lastly, one thing all black Christians should be ready to do for every guilt stricken black mom whom has aborted her child, and for every guilt stricken black dad who has encouraged his partner to abort his child, is to tell them that though abortion is a great sin, it is not an unpardonable sin. We must explain to such men and women that Jesus died for all sin—including the sin of abortion—and if they will

---

[209] Joyce A. Martin, Brady E. Hamilton, Michelle J.K. Osterman, and Anne K. Driscoll, "Births: Final Data for 2018", National Vital Statistics Report, vol. 68, Number 13, November 27, 2019, https://www.cdc.gov/nchs/data/nvsr/nvsr68/nvsr68_13-508.pdf.

but come to Him, God Himself will forgive them of all their sins, and increasingly transform them into the person He wants them to be. We can confidently point guilt stricken black men and women to Christ, because to Him all black lives and souls matter.

# Embodiment and Orality: Methodology Mined from African Diaspora Formed Preaching for the Homiletics Classroom

Jaclyn P. Williams

## Introduction

Preaching formed within the African diaspora experience is imbued with many unique characteristics. There is a certain "something" that speaks to the mind and spirit holistically when Black souls preach the word of God. Black preaching is incarnational preaching. Black preaching is an outpouring of good fruit born of inherent and inherited sensibilities. Ultimately, Black preaching is forged in orality and embodiment.

Proclaimers of God's word preach from God within our bodies amongst the people. As elusive as it may seem, defining embodiment is a centering point in this discussion. It is what preachers are striving for, consciously or subconsciously. The alternative is a compartmentalization that is at best disruptive and at worst destructive. We must be in our body, aware of its resources when proclaiming the revealed word when we preach. So must we be bodily engaged in the story, in the peculiar and particular encounter that the preaching moment becomes. Orality is a manifestation of embodied word, whether that word is the story of a people that encompasses shared beliefs and values, or the self-revelation of the Triune God. God speaks to, and inspires, the whole of creation.

There is a need to set the stage for this study by defining what is meant by embodiment and orality for when speaking of preaching. While embodiment is a broad field, for the purposes of this discourse, embodiment is the tangible manifestation of something that is seemingly intangible. That is to say, embodiment is the whole-being manifestation of being bodied. The mental, emotional and spiritual self are not separate from the body, but rather integration is necessary. The experience of one aspect impacts the experience of the other. Embodiment is also the methods one engages to access the knowledge gained by the body, as well as the methods of expressing with the entirety of the body. Orality is one such method.

Orality is a holistic expression of embodiment, in that the message being shared must first be embodied by the storyteller. Orality is a spoken literature as opposed to a written literature. In the manifestation of African oral tradition, as defined by the International Orality Network, orality is full-body, full-person engagement of self; the listener. Of course, Divinity is the catalyst and sustenance of this engagement, allowing for participation in the communal story on multiple levels.[210] The significance for this study is that preaching is a lived event. It comes to fruition in the encounter between God and the people in the proclaiming moment. It is important to note that Africa is not the only place where orality as an art form is a vital part of the culture. However, Africa is the place of focus for this moment.[211]

---

[210] "What is Orality," *International Orality Network*, accessed March 12, 2021, https://orality.net/about/what-is-orality/. "Before writing was developed, cultures passed along their cultural tradition, including their history, identity, and religion, through their stories, proverbs, poems, songs, riddles, etc. These are all oral art forms; that is, they are spoken, sung or chanted. Purely oral societies pass along everything that matters from one generation to another without putting anything into writing. They rely on the spoken word (including its sung and chanted forms)."

[211] John Miles Foley, "*Introduction*," in *Signs of Orality: The Oral Tradition and Its Influence in the Greek and Roman World*, ed. E. Anne MacKay (Leiden: Brill Academic, 1999), 1- 2.

Embodiment and orality combine to strengthen a holistic process of proclamation. The intentional and practiced integration of the two can bring a lived theology of preaching to the forefront for preachers, learned and novice. With this proposition in mind, a framework of exploration will be built around the following questions.

1. How does embodiment engage with orality training for preachers within the homiletics classroom?
2. How is orality, as defined in this study, a manifestation of embodiment?
3. How does bringing orality and embodiment into the homiletics classroom create culturally significant learning and inclusion within the academy of homiletical study and training?

Since we are talking about Christian preaching, we need to spend a moment talking about Jesus Christ. Although there is a strong heritage of proclamation found in the lives of the prophets, Jesus' homiletical method is the beginning for Christian preachers as it encompasses the entirety of the Gospel foundation.[212] Jesus preached and guided from his spiritual and historical context, operating as an offering of word: "Take it, this is my body."[213] This is a mystical and mysterious vision of the Word offering the body itself as a sacrament. Jesus brought his full self to the moment of preaching, informed by all elements of his life.[214] The Jesus at the

---

[212] Albert R. Bond and Barry L. Davis, *Learning from the Master Preacher* (Dallas, TX: God-Speed Publishing, 2013), 96-99. Bond credits Jesus as being the creator of the Christian pulpit and advocates for the use of the principals that Jesus illustrated as a preacher. Every moment of Christian proclamation since Jesus has been an interpretation of his homiletical method.
[213] Mk. 14:22; unless otherwise noted, all biblical citations are from the New American Standard Bible (NASB).
[214] Williams C. Wilkinson, "*Jesus as Preacher*," in *The Biblical World* 6.6, 476-489 (1895), 476. Wilkinson emphasizes that "it is of himself. It is the natural language of the speaker. Instead of being put on, it is such that it could not even be conceived as put off…In the case of Jesus, the style is he."

moment of proclamation is not separate from the Jesus at rest or in moments of private fellowship. He moved with ease between critical distance from destructive and distorted power structures and empathy with the spiritual, emotional and physical needs of the people.[215] Jesus of Nazareth was a boldly embodied preacher and used a type of orality to bring forth the word. It is from this boldness that we are propelled into our own journey of fully bodied and fully present preaching.

## Ain't Them Bodies Saints

When I speak of embodiment and the body, I am speaking of the physical body as a conduit that informs and enhances relationship. Each area—physiological, sociological, psychological, spiritual and emotional—of how we can experience knowing and how we are known is included in this study's definition of the body. Embodiment is a part of our humanity, our intrapersonal/interpersonal engagement, and a part of how we experience the creation and the Creator. Embodied preaching is unapologetic in taking up the space it is meant to take up. At the same time, embodied preaching is offered with an understanding that this is a communal moment rather than an individual moment of grandstanding.

The process of embodied preaching is a process of exploration and identification that is bolstered by a practice that observes representation and imagination. Stuart Hall says: "It is only through the way in which we represent and imagine ourselves that we come to know how we are constituted and who we are."[216] Holistic personhood finds a home in the

---

[215] Bond and Davis, *Learning from the Master Preacher*, 163. See the outline of Jesus the preacher and the integration of his home life, education, silent years at Nazareth, and consciousness of the divine.

[216] Stuart Hall, "What is This 'Black' in Black Popular Culture?", in *Black Popular Culture*, ed. Michele Wallace and Gina Dent, 29-33 (Seattle, WA: Bay Press, 1992), 29.

body, and the varying levels of engagement are complex.[217] For preaching, this means that something comes to life within the body and can then be offered from that body to the bodies of others. Preachers need a body philosophy and a bodied practice that promotes this kind of fluidity in their homiletical methods. They need a preparation process that is unafraid and unashamed of the body as a source of communion and relationship with God.

Thus we arrive at a definition of preaching as incarnational embodiment. This is an all-inclusive definition that incorporates every moment from inspiration to proclamation and beyond. Through the inspiration and power of the Triune God, word is being formed within the body, prepared for the Body, and proclaimed from the body. The body is the vessel of the labor and deliverance of the word. We can sense intuitively, in our bodies, God's incarnate word, wrapped in flesh, just as much as we can sense it intellectually. The Word is still being made manifest in creation and those who preach are inheritors of the mantle to speak word. Michel Henry's work with phenomenology argues for the created (preachers) to engage with the Creator (God) through intentional as well as pre-intentional means.

> Life "reveals itself" in flesh in a way that no act of thought, philosophical or otherwise can, since it is only by being alive that we know, with an invincible certainty, what life is. In the immanence of life in flesh, all of life's modalities are revealed—as what they are…life in the flesh is real life in real

---

[217] Jacques Derrida, "Violence and Metaphysics", in *Emmanuel Levinas: Beyond Levinas*, ed. Claire Elise Katz and Lara Trout, 88-173 (Abingdon: Routledge 2005), 102. "Body: that is, also exteriority, locality in the fully spatial, literally spatial, meaning of the word; a zero point, the origin of space, certainly, but an origin which has no meaning before the of, an origin inseparable from genitivity and from the space that it engenders and orients: an inscribed origin."

flesh, the life that allows each of us at every moment to say, and say with certainty, "I am alive."[218]

In a homiletical learning environment, the body must be invited to touch the experience of sensing, by engaging in activities that open the self to the possibility and expectation of a bodily knowing of God.[219]

Jakub Urbaniak, in conversation with Henry's philosophy of lived experience revealed in the flesh, adds a vital layer to this pathway of approaching a lived theology of incarnate word. Urbaniak stresses the significance of cultural identification with Christ. Cultural identification informs the processing of self-identification that includes a lived theology of the bodied self. He engages Niels Henrik Gregersen's framework of deep incarnation and a South African Christology outlined by Tinyiko Maluleke. He states: "This 'improvised dialogue' between Maluleke and the deep incarnation theologians stems from my conviction that they have more to offer if their respective insights (whether harmonious or dissonant) on God's radical embodiment in the world are unfolded, not separately, but in relation to each other… Put crudely, while the deep incarnation theologians extend Jesus' body into social and cosmic bodies, Maluleke locates Jesus' body in the bodies of his fellow Africans."[220] In other words, there must be a personally identifiable cultural knowing of Jesus in order to preach a culturally relevant Jesus. Culture is context, and context is key. Preaching students merit an opportunity to make leaps that push against a limited theology of the body in preaching. This is especially true when one

---

[218] Michel Henry, *Incarnation: A Philosophy of Flesh.* (Evanston, IL: Northwestern University Press, 2015), 172.

[219] Jean-Paul Martinon, *After Rwanda: In Search of New Ethics* (Amsterdam: Editions Rodopi, 2013), 124. "The body is therefore not just "in space"; it is also an excess of sense that breaks space. The body is the breaking through (of) the form of the sensible as excess of senses, a breaking through that never reaches a breaking point, not even when it is dying."

[220] Jakub Urbaniak, "Between the Christ of Deep Incarnation and The African Jesus of Tinyiko Maluleke: An Improvised Dialogue," in *Modern Theology* 34.2, 177-205 (2018): 178-179.

considers that these students will be preaching a word that illuminates the limitlessness of God.

## That'll Preach

So, how do we get there? How do we reintegrate our bodies into the process of holistic, embodied preaching? We are created to experience God's revelation through the entirety of our beings. So, why do we only teach to the mind, expecting the body to follow without an overt invitation? African philosopher Anton Wilhelm Amo takes the argument so far as to share that the mind cannot sense and it is the body that is the spirit's instrument: "that the body is made use of on behalf of the subject inhering in it…on behalf of the instrument of its operation and the medium."[221] One pathway to resisting, and perhaps rebuking, a compartmentalized practice of preaching is to introduce orality as a resource.

Tied to oral tradition, orality is the method while oral tradition and literature is the manifestation.[222] Orality illuminates the signs, symbols, beliefs, and values of a community. In the effort to encapsulate the importance of viewing orality as a way of calling and responding, Francis Abiola Irele claims that "functionality in oral literature arises from the very fact that we are dealing with speech acts that are intentional, directed as a consequence toward eliciting a form of response. An oral culture is typically associated with face-to-face situations which facilitate an immediate rapport between social actors. The necessity of communication becomes the very condition of the existence and elaboration at any level of literary form in such a culture."[223] So we have an oral art that utilizes the methods

---

[221] Justin E.H. Smith, *Nature, Human Nature, and Human Difference* (Princeton, NJ: Princeton University Press), 223.

[222] Walter J. Ong, *Orality and Literacy* (New York, NY: Routledge, 2015), 5-10.

[223] Francis Abiola Irele, *Sounds of a Tradition: The Souls of Black Folk* in *The Cambridge History of African American Literature,* ed. M. Graham & J. Ward, Jr., 19-38 (Cambridge: Cambridge University Press, 2011), 29.

of claiming space with a sense of authority, dialogically telling a shared story that expects a response, and building communal rapport in ways that are formative. Do these not sound like aspects that are present within African diaspora preaching traditions? It is that explicitness and the ability to serve the moment of proclamation as a moment of organic lived theology that we are talking about when we identify the importance of orality as a methodology. It is a fruitful resource in bridging the gaps that compartmentalize mind, body, and spirit, as preachers participate in the process of authentically and humbly proclaiming the word of God.

There are five main characteristics of orality that inhabit oral tradition within African cultural behaviors. Three of these characteristics—the phatic, ludic, and aesthetic functions—set the stage in this interconnected literary art form. The other two form the method of artistic application to the message. It is helpful to note that although these characteristics may be formulated in a Westernized thought arena, the inherent ethos of the characteristics are found within African storytelling frameworks and functionality. These traditions can be traced to oral expression that is innate to the preaching of African descended peoples.[224] They have been imprinted into the collective body of Black preaching in the US, and certainly into an approach to the performing arts.[225]

As previously stated, the phatic, ludic, and aesthetic functions set the stage. However, this is not to say that these aspects function

---

[224] James S. Tinney, "The 'Miracle' of Black Preaching," *Christianity Today* 20.9, 14-16 (1976): 14.

[225] Sandra L. Richards, "Function at the Junction"? African Diaspora Studies and Theater Studies," in *African Diaspora and the Disciplines*, ed. Tejumola Olaniyan and James H. Sweet, 193-212 (Bloomington, IN: Indiana University Press, 2010), 195. "Given histories of enslavement, imposed illiteracy, and impoverishment throughout the Americas, the majority of Black people have eschewed the production of drama or verbal, text-based theater. Rather, they have used the body itself and its ability to create music, song, and dance as an archive into which knowledge and value systems could be embedded, remembered, and passed down intergenerationally."

superficially or artificially. Furthermore, the "stage" that is spoken of is the stage of communal knowing. This stage is symbolic of a knitting together that epitomizes the Body of Christ. The phatic function is the psychological connecting point and signifier of social connection and communion. It is this connecting point in Black preaching that acknowledges the inherent relationship between God, preacher and listener.[226] It's the head nod as we pass on the street, the "dap" as we greet one another, and the knowing looks and eyebrow raises passed as communication of camaraderie. The ludic function describes how our senses want to come and play when we are engaged in storytelling and receiving. It is not merely our minds that respond, but rather the entirety of our sensory experience. Our createdness hungers for this.[227] Last of these three, we have the aesthetic function which is where the storyteller artist creates the world for the listeners and says, "imagine with me"[228] and "evokes a collective investment in an aesthetic event."[229]

The first of the two remaining application functions within orality is the didactic function, which says that stories reveal the morality of

---

[226] J. L. Austin, *How To Do Things with Words* (Cambridge, MA: Harvard University Press, 1962); Bronislaw Malinowski, *The Problem of Meaning in Primitive Languages*, Supplement to C. K. Ogden and I. A. Richards, *The Meaning of Meaning* (New York, NY: Harcourt Brace Jovanovich, 1989). See the discussions of Austin and Malinowski concerning the connection between social behavior and the efficacy of communication on social behavior.

[227] Irele, *Sounds of Tradition*, 29. Irele argues that the phatic and ludic functions work together in harmony to create a "palpable form" that is gratifying to all of the senses.

[228] Irele, *Sounds of Tradition*, 30. "Imaginative expression provides a channel to a unique experience of language, one in which language itself comes to be regarded as artifact, as object of aesthetic contemplation. Thus, the aesthetic function reveals the objective nature of language, felt as an entity and therefore capable of being worked upon, molded, manipulated for effect."

[229] Irele, *Sounds of a Tradition*, 30. "This perception of language and the aesthetic function associated with it is well summed up in the Igbo meta-proverb: 'Proverbs are the palm oil with which words are eaten,' a proverb that Chinua Achebe cites to great effect in his novel *Things Fall Apart*. But whereas in written literature the aesthetic function of language relies on the individual response of the reader taken in isolation, in the oral context the pleasure of words is a public good, evoking a collective investment in an aesthetic event."

a culture.²³⁰ Present within this element is the root grounding and core connection that we have a responsibility and privilege to honor the "we" of our community. It is not just for my good but for our good. What are our codes by which we live? How do we hold one another up with these codes?²³¹ With the fifth application we come to the symbolic function. This is where the modality of orality serves to guide in the process of collective self-defining. The conscious and subconscious collective is allowed to cognitively map where we have been, where we are, and where we are going. We are helped to understand the world as we relate to it then, now, and in the future.²³²

In practice, artistic orality training can take on many forms. The core of the pursuit is to engage preaching students in exercises that enhance and challenge their physical and imaginative ability to tell a story from a position of inhabiting the story. This can range from simple storytelling, both verbal and non-verbal, to the creation of narrative frameworks for processing self and communal identity.²³³ For preachers, the story that is being told, is the story of God being revealed to all of creation in a multitude of ways.

A specific example of engaging orality in the homiletics classroom can be found in bringing a jali-inspired storytelling model to the work. Jali are multi-functioning storytellers within many West African communities. They are not mere entertainers. Jali fill a number of professional roles, including orator, praisesinger, arbiter, political

---

[230] Irele, *Sounds of a Tradition*, 31.

[231] Irele, *Sounds of a Tradition*, 31. "This explains the enormous appeal these stories have had for generations of African children and their preservation in the Black Diaspora…for it is in the nature and function of the stories that they serve as a channel of social criticism."

[232] Irele, *Sounds of a Tradition*, 32. "The immediate connection between the symbolic function of oral literature and the historical imagination in Africa can be perceived in the fact that history in the oral tradition is conceived not so much as a faithful reconstruction of the past but rather as a recreation, a reactualization in the present of events in the course of which the original foundation of the collective existence was established. Oral literature thus offers the means for the traditional society to acquire a consciousness of itself."

[233] The author's experience with the Suzuki Actor Training Method and Viewpoints are utilized as source material here.

negotiator, matchmaker, genealogist, historian, ceremonial officiator, and entrepreneur.[234] It follows that within the parameters of this role, there is an enacted connection between the story of the people and the functioning of what this story represents within the larger context of society. Jalis are not functioning as preachers, but they are maintaining some of the cultural import that is maintained by preachers within the Black preaching context. One can see a connection here to the trivocal definition of preaching and the role of the preacher captured by Kenyatta Gilbert:

> African American preaching is a ministry of Christian proclamation—a theo-rhetorical discourse about God's good will toward community with regard to divine intentionality, communal care, and the active practice of hope—that finds resources internal to Black life in the North American context… African American preaching, at all times, absconds its character and charge to the church and the public unless it recovers its elemental prophetic, priestly, and sagely voice.[235]

It is also worth reflecting upon the connections between personal and communal agency, as means of relating to and relaying the continuing incarnated word that God is speaking into creation and into our very bodies. Cultural anthropologist Paulla A. Ebron clarifies the work of the jali in this pursuit:

> The importance of the work of jali in making greatness, first as deed and then as word—that is, history—was instilled in me over and over by my jali informants. One story was particularly helpful in stimulating my understanding of historical agency. Even an ordinary person, perhaps even an undistinguished

---

[234] Paulla A. Ebron, *Performing Africa* (Princeton, NJ: Princeton University Press, 2002), 6.
[235] Kenyatta R. Gilbert *Journey & Promise of African American Preaching* (Minneapolis, MN: Fortress Press, 2011), 11.

young woman, can become a personage in historical narratives she is stimulated to bravery or generosity by the work of jali. She rises from her ordinariness to become the heroine of song and story. When she dies, she is remembered; her greatness, interwoven with that of others, becomes part of the history that jali tell.[236]

Preaching students would not be encouraged to imitate a jali's specific style, but rather to listen to the wisdom of the tradition and how it functions. They would learn through experiential exposure to the jali storytelling methods with two objectives in mind: First, to engage and respond—in body, mind, and spirit—a study of embodied speech and connection to individual and communal formation. Second, to receive the invitation to mine their own spiritual, cultural, social heritage for storyteller lineage. Storytelling, with a wide spectrum of functioning and meaning, is a part of many cultures if you travel back far enough to gather and gain from what has been misplaced and misdirected.[237] Yes, there will be some practical takeaways from the work that may impact sermon delivery, but the main emphasis should be pointed towards integrational formation of self within the process of embodiment of the word. There is good fruit on the vine within our own bodied story with God. Let us commit to the work of harvesting this fruit within the academy, just as we seek to do in the sanctuary. Let us do this work within a framework that strives to illuminate diversity of thought and

---

[236] Ebron, *Performing Africa*, 99-100. Ebron goes on to share about the importance of bestowing historical greatness through the work of the jali. This is not a validated method of recording the historical agency of a people in the majority culture: "Jali remind historians of the importance of the historian—jali or academic—in memorializing greatness, withdrawing it from obscurity, and bringing it into history."

[237] See works such as historian and anthropologist A. G. Velthuizenm's, "On Truth-Telling and Storytelling: Truth-Seeking During Research Involving Communities with an Oral Culture and a History of Violent Conflict," in *The Journal for Transdisciplinary Research in Southern Africa* 10.4 (2014): 19 -35.

experience, theologically and practically. A direct connection to orality and Black preaching is evident.

The purpose here is not to suggest that Black preachers are knowingly relying on these five characteristics of orality. In fact, these are elements of communication tradition that have been, for the most part, passed down through the collective subconscious. As Ralph Ellison puts it:

> Folklore ... offers the first drawings of any group's character. It preserves mainly those situations [that] have repeated themselves again and again in the history of any given group. It describes those rites, manners, customs, and so forth, which ensure the good life, or destroy it; and it describes those boundaries of feeling, thought, and action [that] that a particular group has found to be the limitations of the human condition. It projects this wisdom in symbols [that] express the group's will to survive; it embodies those values by which the group lives and dies. These drawings may be crude but they are nonetheless profound in that they represent the group's attempt to humanize the world.[238]

From Africa, through the middle passage, to the hush harbors on antebellum plantations and landing in contemporary barber and beauty shops and sanctified sanctuaries, these roots are deep and their reach is wide.[239] Acknowledging the import and allowing the inclusion within the homiletical training ethos confesses the necessity of culturally competent and inclusive process of cultivation. Orality, in

---

[238] Hazel Arnett Ervin, "Collective Unconscious," in *The Handbook of African American Literature* (Gainesville, TN: Gainesville University Press, 2004), 172.

[239] Vorris Nunley, *Keepin' It Hushed: The Barbershop and African American Hush Harbor Rhetoric* (Detroit, MI: Wayne State University Press, 2011), 23. Black informal spaces were and are survival spaces for the Black publicly engaged psyche: "In these spaces, enslaved Africans and African Americans can come in from the wilderness of the racially mediated public sphere... [they are] refuges that warded off Black social death."

its celebration of communalized storytelling and story-making, is an entry into allowing the word of God to inhabit the space of the body and bring it alive in all senses for teller and listener.

## That'll Teach

People love Black preaching. It is a generality, but it is true. The reasons are varied, spanning the socio-political spectrum from true engagement and thoughtful discernment to entertainment and even to fetishizing.[240] Although Black preaching culture is by no means monolithic, there is something that touches the veil between one realm of experiencing God and the next in many of its manifestations. While this is not exclusive to Black preaching, it does shows up in Black preaching and culture in distinct ways. There is something in the DNA of Black preaching that hearkens back to the pre-enslavement experience of oral literature and the psychic resonance of orality. These roots extend across time and space, connecting certain aspects of this broad while specific preaching tradition to the oral traditions of Africa.[241]

---

[240] Simone C. Drake and Dwan K. Henderson, *Are You Entertained* (Durham, NC: Duke University Press, 2020), 1-2. "Perhaps more than at any time in history and more visibly because lives are so technologically intertwined in real time, the "popular" in Black popular cultural productions is commodified, consumed, appropriated, and then, often, mass-produced with startling simultaneity through the very lens that Glover references, as if "white people … know everything about Black culture." See also further comments in Joseph Andrew Johnson's, *The Soul of the Black Preacher* (Cleveland, OH: Pilgrim Press, 1971), 152. Johnson articulates how the elevation of Black preaching, culturally and in the academy, would have necessitated the elevation of Black people and "The white American cultural ego would not permit this."

[241] James S. Tinney, "The 'Miracle' of Black Preaching," in *Christianity Today* 20.9, 12-15 (1976): 14. "Although the Black sermon has distinctively Christian components, its best parallels are to be found in the African 'grist,' the blues, the poetry and folk tales of the African diaspora in America; It [Black preaching] forms a special genre of oral literature that goes beyond the usual categories of white homiletics, and that opens up to an even larger realm of subtle chemistries of art and style found only in Black churches." See also, Henry H. Mitchell, *Black Preaching: The Recovery of a Powerful Art* (Nashville, TN: Abingdon Press, 1990), 23. Mitchell argues that the "disconnected series of contacts between the Christian gospel and African men and women caught up in the Black experience of slavery and oppression" manifested as a formational aspect of Black preaching and also impacts the delivery methods and the response of Black congregations.

We have touched upon elements—embodiment and orality—that would enhance homiletical experiential learning. In addition, we need to understand the cultural importance of this kind of educational approach. Explicit acknowledgement of the validity of these elements as not only trustworthy but also teachable is imperative. If you love our preaching, bring our epistemological import to the classroom. This will facilitate tapping into the senses of personhood that are often ignored in the academy. This will also facilitate spiritual and sermonic inspiration, formation, and transformation with a deeper level of intentionality. Without this acknowledgement, the love of Black preaching exacerbates elements of the magical negro trope, looking to the Black experience for spiritual guidance, and not recognizing and engaging the meaning of the full realization of Black people and life.[242] Certainly, a lived and embodied practice benefits the entirety of the Body of Christ by creating space for a lived theology, on its feet in the classroom. However, for the Black Church and the Black classroom there is an opportunity to illuminate and honor inherent manifestations of storying our beliefs and values. This opportunity leads to a reintegration of a dissected communal identity that reflects the image of God.

Cultural inclusion is imperative within any progression that claims to re-present God and represent the entirety of Creation and its manifestations of personhood. This calls for learning environments that are culturally, ethnically, racially, and linguistically diverse, culturally congruent, culturally appropriate, culturally responsive and culturally compatible.[243] This means assessing and implementing the specific characteristics and models of orality and facilitating the students'

---

[242] Cerise L Glen and Landra J. Cunningham, "The Power of Black Magic: The Magical Negro and White Salvation in Film," in *Journal of Black Studies* 40.2, 135-152 (2009): 142-143. See discussion of the magical negros as spiritually gifted and guiding, yet not a fully-realized character.

[243] Gloria Ladson-Billings, *The Dreamkeepers: Successful Teachers of African American Children* (Hoboken, NJ: John Wiley & Sons, 2009), 17–18.

engagement with methods as a practice, meant to enable the embodied telling of the unraveling story of God and humanity.

## Conclusion

Along with a sound preparation and proclamation process, buoyed by critical exegesis and humble communion with God's spirit, preaching is a practice of lived theology. Homiletics should be taught as such. This kind of teaching necessitates more attention to embodiment, dynamic incarnational awareness through orality, and culturally significant exploration. When preachers are challenged to mine their own cultural identities for entries into innovative ways of receiving and proclaiming incarnate word, God's beauty of creativity and diversity is made manifest. It is vital to bring the ammonia of the sermon and sermonizer out, to use the terminology of Howard Thurman.[244] The physical place of the body is the home of our spiritual, emotional and mental internalization of our relationship with God, self, and others. It needs to be invited to the process of incarnate preaching. Preaching, taught as a practice that incorporates embodiment methods such as orality and cultural substantiation, along with sound exegesis and the Holy Spirit, is vital and necessary. This kind of pedagogical paradigm shift can be the bridge between a theology of preaching and a lived theology of incarnate word. It can facilitate the hope that the word will echo from God to the preacher, to the people, and to all of creation.

---

[244] Thurman, Howard, "Dilemmas of Religious Professional (IV) (Hester Lecture) [Side B], 1971 Feb 12," Pitts Theology Library, Emory University, *The Howard Thurman Digital Archive*, accessed June 28, 2021, https://thurman.pitts.emory.edu/items/show/249. Thurman arrives at the heart of the matter, as it pertains to the spirit and method of preaching: "The sermon is not a lecture…not merely an academic or intellectual exercise for the mind; it is not a commonplace homily that lulls into quiescence or sedation; no--the sermon must always have the smell of ammonia about it. It must be vital and contagious."

# An Onramp to Economic Shalom: Lessons from the Book of Ruth

### Luke Brad Bobo

Ask most Christians what the word *shalom* means and most will say *peace*. Semantically, that definition for shalom is correct but it is also woefully inadequate. For God's academy of Old Testament prophets—enforcers of the covenant—would say that shalom carried a more robust meaning. According to Cornelius Plantinga, shalom is the "universal flourishing, wholeness, and delight—a rich state of affairs in which natural needs are satisfied and natural gifts fruitfully employed."[245] Implied in this definition is the idea that shalom is a state of wholeness or sound health. Shalom then includes sound physical, spiritual, existential, mental, and *economic* health. Shalom includes both God's intention and God's promise of complete realization.

An onramp to economic shalom or health presumes a flourishing economy, "one that respects the freedom and dignity of all, that offers all opportunities for the deployment and exchange of their talents, and that is safeguarded by the rule of law—so that fair play reigns and all people have the opportunity to become self-supporting."[246]

---

[245] Cornelius Plantinga, *Not the Way It's Supposed to Be: A Breviary of Sin*, (Grand Rapids, MI: Eerdmans, 1995), 10.
[246] Amy Sherman, personal message to author, August 21, 2018.

A flourishing and just economy is "one that frees people to do good."[247] Economic shalom then requires that all people—regardless of ethnicity, nationality, gender, race, religion, age or sexual orientation—have the opportunity to become self-supporting. An onramp to such shalom requires all people have the opportunity to exercise human agency by fruitfully employing their natural gifts in the economy. Along with opportunity, economic shalom must also include access, relationship, mutuality, and equity.

An approach to the onramp for economic flourishing occurs quite simply when those who are unemployed, poor, and destitute are granted the opportunity to participate in the economy by deploying their God-given skills and abilities. The godly deployment of human and material assets not only serves as the beginning step toward restoring the "economic dignity"[248] of able-bodied workers but this deployment also serves to steer *imago Dei* bearers toward an onramp to economic shalom or wholeness.

Central to the economy is not invisible hands; rather, inherently core to the economy is virtuous *imago Dei* bearers who are allowed to make themselves useful, because it is through work that "we make ourselves useful to others."[249] *Imago Dei* bearers, who are permitted to participate unhindered in the economy, will experience what abolitionist Frederick Douglass experienced as a free man in New Bedford, MA. Douglass said this after landing his first job: "It swelled my heart as I clasped this money, realizing that I had no master…that my hands were my own."[250] Douglass' heart bulged because he was

---

[247] Karen Swallow Prior, *On Reading Well: Finding the Good Life through Great Books*, (Grand Rapids, MI: Brazos, 2018), 70.

[248] Michael Gerson, Stephanie Summers, & Katie Thompson, *Unleashing Opportunity: Why Escaping Poverty Requires a Shared Vision of Justice*, (Beaver Falls, PA: Fall City Press, 2015), 111.

[249] Lester DeKoster, *Work: The Meaning of Your Life: A Christian Perspective,* 2nd ed., (Grand Rapids, MI: Christian Library Press, 2010), 1.

[250] David Blight, *Frederick Douglass: Prophet of Freedom*, (New York, NY: Simon & Schuster, 2018), 91.

given access to the onramp to economic shalom through the work of his own agency and the work of his own hands, heart, and head. This renowned orator's heart ballooned because he knew that our work is essentially a gift of self—endowed with abilities from God—to the service of others.

How might the church assist in directing people trapped in systems of poverty to this onramp to economic shalom? I believe the answer is found in distinguishing the difference between two prepositions: to and with. Charity work is done *to* a person in need. This *to*-service is customarily unidirectional and can engender an unhealthy dependency. I submit working or doing *with* a person in need is best, dignifying, and is much more sustainable and creates lasting change.[251]

This paper considers an Old Testament practice: gleaning. Found in the book of Ruth, this book illustrates the merits of *doing with* instead of *doing to* those in economic peril. Ruth, a vulnerable person, is afforded an opportunity to deploy her God-given abilities and skills for entry to the onramp toward economic shalom. In other words, Ruth had assets, where an asset is a useful or valuable thing, person, or quality. The chief asset that Ruth had at her disposal was the ability to engage in able-bodied work.

In the book of Ruth, we see that the godly deployment of human and material assets not only serves as the beginning step toward restoring the "economic dignity" of Ruth and her aged mother-in-law, Naomi, but this deployment also serves to steer these *imago Dei* bearers toward an onramp to economic shalom or wholeness.[252] Can what we learn from this ancient book to help the unemployed, poor, and destitute advance toward economic shalom of our day? I believe the answer is a resounding and unequivocal yes. A brief look at this ancient practice, gleaning, is basic to this affirmative response.

---

[251] Stefenie Sawyer, personal message to author, September 22, 2020.
[252] Gerson, Summers, & Thompson, *Unleashing Opportunity*, 111.

## Ruth: Socio-Economically Destitute Foreigner

The story of Ruth[253] is familiar to us. The patriarch of the family, Elimelech, migrates from Bethlehem, the house of bread, to the foreign ground of the Moabites. Calamity strikes the Elimelech home. Elimelech, the breadwinner and provider, dies. Naomi's two sons, Mahlon and Chilion, die, leaving bereft Naomi a bitter widow, without protection, and with two widowed daughters-in-law, Moabites Orpah and Ruth.[254] After a teary good-bye, Orpah returns to the home of her kin. Ruth, however, promises Naomi: "Don't plead with me to abandon you or to return and not follow you. For wherever you go, I will go, and wherever you live, I will live; your people will be my people, and your God will be my God."[255] With these words, Ruth binds herself to her bereft and bitter mother-in-law, Naomi. As womanist theologian Renita Weems honestly points out, "Ruth's words are so uncompromising in their commitment, so resolute in their pledge, they embarrass us."[256] However, this type of commitment is not unique to sisters only. Brothers, David and Jonathan, shared a similar uncompromising commitment to each other.

Naomi and Ruth, both bereft women, both vulnerable, return to Bethlehem during the barley harvest season.[257] Ruth, who is noble, virtuous, and abled-bodied, is not idle; rather, she searches for work so that she can provide for herself and her mother-in-law. Divine

---

[253] The book of Ruth is considered a short story, a novella or romance. This book is read at Jewish festivities along with Esther, Ecclesiastes, Lamentations and Song of Songs.

[254] Ruth 1:1-5; unless otherwise noted, all biblical citations are from the Christian Standard Bible (CSB).

[255] Ruth 1:16.

[256] Renita J. Weems, *Just A Sister Away: A Womanist Vision of Women's Relationships in the Bible*, (San Diego, CA: LuraMedia, 1988), 28.

[257] Ruth 1:22.

providence, not luck, leads Ruth to the fields of kinsman Boaz. It is here that we see Boaz' generosity on full display as he goes well beyond the letter of the gleaning laws.[258]

## Gleaning Law

The gleaning law teaches us that we already have resources to bless our neighbors. Appropriating the Old Testament gleaning law is a wonderful way to love our neighbors as Rabbi Jesus commanded in Matthew 22:34-40. This love for neighbor is sacrificial, costly, other-centered, and generous.

The gleaning law was a key ingredient of God's welfare plan for the most vulnerable in the ancient Near East. Adhering to the gleaning law was costly for the landowner. The Mosaic Law required field, vineyard, and orchard owners not to gather what was left behind after reaping; rather, reapers were mandated to leave some for the economically and socially disadvantaged to harvest for their sustenance. According to Zechariah 7:10, there were four categories of the economically and socially disadvantaged—the orphan, widow, poor, and foreigner (or resident alien).

The Pentateuch summoned God's people, his redeemed-once-enslaved people to care for these economically and socially disadvantaged persons. For example, we read:

> When you reap the harvest of your land, you are not to reap all the way to the edges of your field or gather the gleanings of your harvest. You shall not pick your vineyard bare or gather the fallen fruit of your vineyard; you shall leave them for the poor and the stranger: I am the Lord your God. [259]

---

[258] Ruth 2-3.
[259] Lev. 19:9-10.

And we also read these words,

> When you reap the harvest in your field and overlook a sheaf in the field, do not turn back to get it; it shall go to the stranger, the fatherless, and the widow—in order that the Lord your God may bless you in all your undertakings. When you beat down the fruit of your olive trees, do not go over them again; that shall go to the stranger, the fatherless, and the widow. When you gather the grapes of your vineyard, do not pick it over again; that shall go to the stranger, the fatherless, and the widow. Always remember that you were a slave in the land of Egypt; therefore, do I enjoin you to observe this commandment.[260]

This latter passage provides the Israelites with the motive to care for these economically and socially disadvantaged persons as God reminds them, they once occupied the low estate of a slave in the land of Egypt and God generously provided for and rescued them. God rescued the Israelites from horrific and inhumane working conditions and from a capricious supervisor, Pharaoh. In other words: "God's law instructed his people to love the sojourner and the poor [and the widow and the orphan] as a reflection of his love for them."[261] Similarly, Christians know that they too were once residents of the kingdom of darkness, enslaved to their sin and to Satan, a capricious master. However, now we are free from this tyranny, and called to tangibly love the poor, widow, sojourner, and orphan.

The book of Ruth beautifully depicts Boaz, a landowner who obeyed this agricultural law and what it cost him. According to the Pentateuch, Ruth met three of the four categories of need—she was poor, a widow, and a foreigner. She was socially and economically destitute. So, by allowing Ruth to work for her sustenance, Boaz was

---

[260] Deut. 24:19-22.
[261] Benjamin T. Quinn & Walter R. Strickland II, *Every Walking Hour: An Introduction to Work and Vocation for Christians* (Bellingham, MA: Lexham Press, 2016), 28.

obeying his God who is generous. Boaz imitates God by practicing generosity. Additionally, by obeying this law he was also preserving Ruth's dignity, because as an *imago Dei* bearer, she was created to work.[262] Instead of giving her a material handout, Boaz allows Ruth, a foreigner, to work with her hands to provide for her and her mother-in-law. The Theology of Work (TOW) Commentary on Ruth says this: "This gleaning law allowed the unemployed to work with his hands to provide for his family. Boaz could have had grain delivered to the home of Ruth and Naomi. On the contrary, Boaz allowed this foreigner to work with her hands and image God by working."[263] The TOW Commentary goes on to say: "The process—allowing Ruth to glean or to work—preserved her dignity, made use of her skills and abilities, freed her and Naomi from long-term dependency, and made them less vulnerable to exploitation."[264]

Contrary to popular belief, many unemployed people in our culture are not looking for a handout; but rather, many are looking for an opportunity to image God by working with their hands, to deploy their natural God-given gifts. They are simply counting on the generosity of believers to use their material and immaterial resources of power and influence to grant them access to opportunity.[265] Ruth's gleaning continues for a period of up to seven weeks because of Boaz's generosity. Because Boaz went above the call of Lev. 19:9-10, he suffered a great financial loss.[266] Boaz's generosity allowed Ruth and her bereaved mother-in-law, Naomi to survive.

This Old Testament gleaning law fits well with one of Made to Flourish's economic wisdom principles: "The most effective way to

---

[262] Gen. 1:26-28; Eph. 2:8-10.
[263] "Introduction to the book of Ruth," Theology of Work Project, accessed July 8, 2021, https://www.theologyofwork.org/old-testament/ruth-and-work/.
[264] Theology of Work Project, "Introduction to the book of Ruth."
[265] Quinn & Strickland, *Every Walking Hour*, 28.
[266] Jerram Barrs, *Through His Eyes: God's Perspective On Women in The Bible* (Wheaton, IL: Crossway, 2009), 140.

turn around poverty, economic distress, and injustice is by expanding opportunity for people to develop and deploy their God-given productive potential in communities of exchange."[267] By allowing Ruth to glean in his fields, Boaz helped Ruth to overcome poverty and economic distress. Boaz's obedience to the Mosaic law greatly aided a human family (and future generations). His obedience allowed Ruth access to the onramp toward economic shalom for her and Naomi. Today, we operate within the abundance of grace, and like Boaz, and have opportunity to surpass every legal expectation for the good of our neighbors.

## What Did Boaz and Ruth Know?

Ruth and Boaz were human instruments to usher Ruth and Naomi, two widows, onto the onramp toward economic shalom. What did Boaz and Ruth know? Ruth, the primary breadwinner for Naomi's household, knew four things.

First, although she was vulnerable as a widowed foreign woman, Ruth knew she still had an obligation to serve the vulnerable, her mother-in-law. Ruth had assets that Naomi did not. Ruth had the desire, tenacity, and ability to work; Naomi did not. As Alicia Besa Panganiban eloquently explains, Ruth had to be audacious and resilient "amidst her own vulnerability."[268] This resiliency, common among many oppressed and marginalized people groups—the disabled, African-Americans, women, immigrants, Native Americans— "was rooted in *hesed* (a loving kindness, a generosity beyond the call of duty)."[269]

---

[267] Luke Bobo, *Whatever You Do: Six Foundations for An Integrated Life*, (Overland Park, KS: Made to Flourish, 2019), 86.
[268] Alicia Besa Panganiban, "Theology of Resilience Amidst Vulnerability in the Book of Ruth," in *Feminist Theology* 28.2, 182-197 (2020): 182.
[269] Panganiban, "Theology of Resilience," 182.

Second, Ruth knew what the widow in 2 Ki. 4:1-7 discovered. Ruth knew that she had to cooperate with God. In other words, lasting and sustainable relief occurs when those *with* assets cooperate *with* God and work *with* the persons in distress to arrive at a sustainable solution. Certainly, there is a place for charity or giving to those in distress (during the COVID-19 pandemic, for example). However, *doing with* those who are in distress preserves the dignity of both giver and receiver, leading to lasting personal and communal change.

Instead of Boaz giving harvested crops to Ruth, he invited her to work for her sustenance because God had endowed her with gifts and assets—she was able-bodied. Boaz, a man with assets such as his field, collaborated *with* Ruth, a woman who was able-bodied, to work his fields. The result? Ruth provided for herself and her mother-in-law.

Third, Ruth knew that to show loving-kindness or *hesed* meant not only a stubborn loyalty to her mother-in-law, but it also meant trusting her mother-in-law. Norton postulates that by instructing Ruth to, "wash, put on perfumed oil, and wear your best clothes. Go down to the threshing floor, but don't let the man know you are there until he has finished eating and drinking. When he lies down, notice the place where he's lying, go in and uncover his feet, and lie down. Then he will explain to you what you should do" that she could have "left Ruth vulnerable not only to sexual violence but also to further social ostracizing."[270] Norton believes "Ruth is literally laid down as a sacrifice for the social mobility of Naomi."[271] Norton believes like Fulata Lusungu Moyo that Ruth, a naive and "a beautiful young foreign woman, had to sell her body to a man old enough to be her father so that her mistress (Naomi) could gain her dignity through restored property."[272] That theory would

---

[270] Yolanda Norton, "Silenced Struggles for Survival: Finding Life in Death in the Book of Ruth," in *I Found God in Me: A Womanist Biblical Hermeneutics Reader*, ed. Mitzi J. Smith, (Eugene, OR: Cascade), 275.

[271] Norton, *Silenced Struggles for Survival*, 275.

[272] Fulata Lusungu Moyo. "'Traffic Violations': Hospitality, Foreignness, and Exploitation: A Contextual Biblical Study of Ruth," in *Journal of Feminist Studies in Religion* 32.2, 83-94 (2016), 87.

have been correct; however, Boaz had already shown Ruth that he was a noble and honorable man by extending her a welcome to glean in his fields and by ordering his workers not to touch her.[273] He lived up to being a "prominent man of noble character."[274] And Naomi knew this about Boaz. In other words, Ruth trusted her mother-in-law and willingly participates in Naomi's plan.

Fourth, Ruth knew the principle of reciprocity. Ruth treated her grieving mother-in-law, Naomi, with loving-kindness, or *hesed*, because Ruth and Orpah had been treated with loving kindness from Naomi and her two sons. The virtue of *hesed* had been passed on to Ruth, who habituated this virtue, and so treated Naomi with loving kindness. Ruth's practice of *hesed* toward Naomi not only marks her acceptance of Yahweh but it also "indicates her acculturation to Israelite life."[275]

Boaz, the gracious landowner, knew four things. First, Boaz (and Ruth) knew their biblical anthropology. Both Boaz and Ruth knew that Ruth was an *imago Dei* bearer that God had endowed with skills and the ability to work, because to image God is to work. Boaz was aware of the import of Gen.1-2, the prologue to the Bible.[276] In Gen. 1-2, we are introduced to a striking and surprising revelation of God. We are not introduced to God as King, God as Warrior, God as Judge, or God as Redeemer. Rather, in this prologue we are introduced to *God as worker*. God works and ceases from work or, He rests (Gen. 2:1-3). The word for *work*, mentioned three times in Gen. 2:1-3, means work as something done or made, and as something quite ordinary.

---

[273] Ruth 2:8-9.

[274] Ruth 2:1.

[275] Panganiban, "Theology of Resilience," 189.

[276] Gen. 1-2 describes God's six-day work week: "[The author's] main interest is telling us that God made the material world as a place for mankind to live: to love, to work, to enjoy and to worship God. The exalted tone of the passage allows the reader to ponder this with a sense of awe, adoring the goodness, power and creativity of the One who did all this," Jack Collins, *Genesis 1-4: A Linguistic, Literary, and theological Commentary*, (Phillipsburg, NJ: P&R Publishing, 2006), 78-79.

Specifically, the word for work ($m^e$ la kah) in Gen. 2:1-3 is used of God's work in creation, of men working with leather (Lev. 13:48, 51), work in the field (1 Chron. 27:26), of a potter's work (Jer. 18:3), of Nehemiah's work on the wall (Neh. 4:5) and the work of priests (2 Chron. 29:34).[277] Boaz and Elisha knew that all work, except sinful work, was sacred. And all work mattered in God's economy.

As those made in his image, we were created to worship, and the work we do becomes an expression of a meaningful life before God. We are like God functionally and ontologically. Ontologically, we are like God because we are moral, affectional, relational, and rational. Functionally, we are like God because we create, manage, rule, subdue, have dominion, work, and rest. So then, to not work is to suffer from a "dignity deficit" because there is dignity in work and because we were made to work.[278] Imagine the plight of the disabled, also *imago Dei* bearers, who cannot physically work. Still God has called his people to engage their imaginations to find humane solutions for these dear people. We are called not to look at these dear people as charity cases or deficient ones. Rather, we must look at them as Boaz looked at Ruth and Naomi—that is, through a creational lens. By looking at them through this lens—through the beauty of creation (before the Fall of Man)—Boaz saw *imago Dei* bearers with something to *bring to the table*. By not reducing Ruth to a mere charity case, Boaz was "seeing her rightly, [which] is a form of justice."[279] Ruth was penniless, but she had something to contribute.[280]

Second, Boaz was powerful; yet he did not abuse his power. Yolanda Norton who asserts "that the book of Ruth was intended to serve the

---

[277] F. Brown, S. Driver, & C. Briggs, *The Brown-Driver-Briggs Hebrew and English Lexicon*, (Peabody, MA: Hendrickson, 1997), 521-522.

[278] "Dignity Deficit: This Way Up," Arthur Brooks, accessed July 9, 2021, https://www.aei.org/spotlight-panels/dignity-deficit-this-way-up.

[279] Prior, *On Reading Well*, 81.

[280] Work is more about contribution than compensation. See Gen. 2 where Adam and Eve *contribute* to the maintenance or upkeep of the garden of Eden.

purposes of normative power structures" and that Boaz's actions were "embedded oppositional forces."[281] However, Boaz does not enforce this normative power structure. Boaz knew that Naomi and Ruth, both widows, belonged to a "precarious social status."[282] There are no "embedded oppositional forces" at play in Boaz's actions. Boaz knew the law of God; and Boaz knew his God. Along with orphans and immigrants, widows were the most needy and powerless who lacked status, respect, and were easy prey for the powerful and unscrupulous.[283] In fact, Boaz specifically and proactively, tells Ruth: "Listen to me, daughter. Do not go to glean in another field. Do not go elsewhere but stay here close. Keep your eyes on the field they are reaping and follow them. I have ordered the men not to molest you."[284] Notice, he ordered his young men not to touch her or sexually abuse her. Boaz and Elisha knew that this unnamed widow and Ruth were economically depressed and vulnerable because of their gender and low social-economic status.

Third, Boaz was *figuratively* acquainted with the spirit of Jeremiah's letter to the exiles in the pagan city, Babylon, and its implications. Specifically, they remembered to "seek the welfare of the city to which I have exiled you and pray to the Lord on its behalf; for in its prosperity, you shall prosper."[285] Jeremiah is alluding to the principle of mutuality. Dr. Martin Luther King Jr., writing from the Birmingham Jail, explains: "We are caught in an inescapable network of mutuality, tied in a single garment of destiny. Whatever affects one directly, affects all indirectly."[286] Boaz (and Ruth) instinctively knew this principle of

---

[281] Norton, "Silenced Struggles," 265.

[282] Donald Gowan, "Wealth and Poverty in the Old Testament: The Case of the Widow, the Orphan, and the Sojourner," in *Interpretation: A Journal of Bible and Theology*, 41.4, 341-353 (1987), 347.

[283] Tokunboh Adeyemo, *Africa Bible Commentary*, (Nairobi: HippoBooks, 2006), 446.

[284] Ruth 2:8-9.

[285] Jer. 29:7.

[286] Martin Luther King Jr., "Letter from the Birmingham City Jail" in *A Testament of Hope: The Essential Writings and Speeches of Martin Luther King Jr.*, ed. James M. Washington, 289-302 (New York, NY: HarperCollins, 1986), 290.

mutuality. They understood well that their flourishing could not be detached from the flourishing of all parties—Ruth, Naomi, and Boaz.

Fourth, and finally, Boaz knew the Pentateuch, especially Lev. 19:9-10. Boaz knew that the book of Leviticus is chiefly a book about holy living before God. And he knew that holy living was not relegated to how one worships only. Holy living encompasses all of life. For example, "holy living means generously caring for those in need."[287] And Ruth and Naomi certainly met the qualifications for those in need.

## Conclusion

God loves his broken, imperfect church. God has uniquely equipped his bride to help alleviate poverty imaginatively, humanely, and biblically to grant the poor an onramp toward economic shalom. Failure to pivot and heed the lessons learned from this Old Testament book will sadly cast the church as an accomplice in perpetuating generational poverty rather than an alleviator of generational poverty. May the church of Jesus Christ heed the four lessons outlined below as she works to bring those on the *margins* of the economy to the *center* of the economy.

One, the church, the pillar and foundation of the truth and the virtue training school, must be vigilant to assure that a flourishing economy, operates by the virtues of love, justice, and truth.[288] Therefore, the church must keep close watch and act to assure that economic shalom includes the benefits of access, relationship, mutuality, and equity for all people.

Two, those we help are preeminently *imago Dei* bearers. They are not charity or goodwill cases. They are not to be viewed as those who are deficient or less-than. Every *imago Dei* bearer has been crowned with "royal dignity" and has something to offer because God has created us with natural gifts to employ—natural gifts to make ourselves

---

[287] Jay Sklar, *Leviticus*, Volume 3, (Downers Grove, IL: IVP, 2014), 245.
[288] 1 Tim. 3:15.

useful to others.[289] Again, may the church "see people rightly" as first, *imago Dei* bearers.[290]

Three, may the church understand that many trapped in systems of poverty are not looking for a *handout*; rather, they are looking for a *hand up*. The poor want to be afforded opportunities to deploy their natural gifts and abilities, endowed by their Creator. They want to contribute, for to contribute is to belong. The church should remember the words of Anthony Emerson: "To give everyone a job and to have a unique role in the community does huge amounts in terms of self-esteem, a sense of personal mission and identity, as well as a sense of belonging. That's a huge part of flourishing."[291]

And lastly, may the church see herself as a "community asset."[292] Jonathan Brooks, pastor of Canaan Community Church, Englewood, IL, challenges the church to see herself as "a partner to all the community leaders and organizations that desire to see [a] community flourish."[293] A church's most significant asset are the people in the pews who have influence, skills, and access. Churches must take an inventory of her assets and then deploy these assets generously. Following this discovery of assets, churches should seek to do ministry *with* others. Like Boaz combined his assets *with* Ruth's assets to arrive at a sustainable solution, the church is in the position to do likewise.

Bryan Stevenson, founder of the Equal Justice Initiative in Montgomery, AL, learned this simple but profound lesson from his grandmother: "You can't understand most of the important things from a

---

[289] Vincent Bacote, *The Political Disciple: A Theology of Public Life*, (Grand Rapids, MI: Zondervan, 2015), 41.

[290] Prior, *On Reading Well*, 81.

[291] RuthAnne Jenkins, "Welcome to Brookwood, Where Good things Grow," *Common Good Magazine*, April 2020, 15.

[292] Jonathan Brooks, *Church Forsaken: Practicing Presence in Neglected Neighborhoods*, (Downers Grove, IL: IVP, 2018), 60.

[293] Brooks, *Church Forsaken*, 60.

distance. You have to *get close*."²⁹⁴ To accurately identify the assets of those we want to serve or help means we must "get close." We must "get close" and listen to those we want to do ministry *with*; because doing ministry *with* others not only honors the dignity of the other but it prevents churches from adopting a top-down patriarchal demeanor.

Boaz and Ruth knew that when two parties with assets collaborate something beautiful and more enduring happens: "Survival, true survival of the body and soul, requires creativity, freedom of thought, *collaboration*. You might have time and I might have land. You might have ideas and I might have strength. You might have a tomato and I might have a knife. *We need each other*."²⁹⁵ When the church does ministry *with* the community or persons in need, not only does this lead to an entry on the onramp toward economic shalom but a sustainable solution is more likely the result.

In sum, Boaz and Ruth knew the power of a village or community. Boaz and Ruth knew the *power of we* as poet Ebony Kearney beautifully illustrates in her poem, "We".²⁹⁶

We

Reflections of self through and through
I am you and you are me
Never forgetting you're no better than me, & I'm no better than you
Because WE are here created equally
Projecting lights for the young to see
Giving HOPE for the young minded
It's our common goal
Because we like-minded …
COMMUNITY

---

²⁹⁴ Bryan Stevenson, *Just Mercy: A Story of Justice and Redemption*, (New York, NY: Spiegel & Grau, 2014), 11.
²⁹⁵ Clemantine Wamariya, *The Girl Who Smiled Beads: A Story of War and What Comes After*, (New York, NY: Penguin Random House, 2018), 177.
²⁹⁶ Ebony Kearney, personal email message to author, October 1, 2020.

Cuz we want our babies to grow up too!
But they need Protection
And a whole Lotta love and affection ... from YOU...
COMMUNITY

We need to plant those tiny seeds of a foundation ... for the COMMUNITY
So, WE can AWAKEN a part of the mind that seeks no limitations ...
Learning that family comes in many forms just take a look, it's the new norm ...
COMMUNITY

Building community requires a WE mentality
Cuz it's a Commitment...
your struggle is my struggle and your joys are my joys ... no resentment!
So, you either with it or against it!
Because WE are creating a solid foundation for OUR future generations to see...

That there is no me without WE.

WE are the COMMUNITY ... The time is Now to Rise Up and bring the UNITY

# Ujamaa: Sacred Work in a Whole New World

## Jacqueline Dyer

Welcome to Ujamaa: Sacred Work. We are in an unprecedented time—not just because of the 2020 social, political and medical upheavals—but because we decided to do an unprecedented thing—to make a space dedicated to discussions and scholarship of Gospel Haymanot or Orthodox Gospel from an African diasporic perspective. This is not the creation of a branch of theology that was popularized in the eras of Western/European empires and colonizations. In fact, if you trace the places where Jesus and his people lived and traveled, parts of northern Africa and the Middle East, you will find several things. First, a blue-eyed Jesus with white skin and similar parents would not have been able to hide in ancient Egypt for several years when Jesus was young, because of the darker skin of the indigenous people. Second, all the history recorded in the Bible occurred in these regions through the indigenous people. Third, the people intermingled with other groups in the region since the beginning of humanity. An example of this was the marriage of Joseph and the African woman, Asenath, whose two sons—Ephraim and Manasseh—were adopted by Israel to be one of the twelve tribes that eventually swelled to be thousands strong before they left Egypt in Africa. The Israelites should be identified as a people of color. None of these people were "white":

European Christians, from the Iberians through the British, saw themselves as agents of positive, if not divine, change, as it were, the markers of creaturely contingency. They saw themselves as those ordained to enact a providential transition. In so doing they positioned themselves as those first conditioning their world rather than being conditioned by it.[297]

Gospel Haymanot is a reclamation of what has been obscured for centuries by those who conscripted the lands, people, information and histories, hailing from these warmer climes for their own purposes, rebranding them as things populated by, discovered by and somehow enlightened by cultural overlays from their own regions.

We are attempting to be part of a great wind that God is stirring to blow off the layers of centuries of reconstruction, and to resurrect and remove the grave clothes from our faith-history—a history that doesn't need to be reinvented, just more accurately remembered. I am grateful to be a part of this effort and humbled at the same time. This is sacred work. Throughout the Bible—Old Testament and New—there are stories of resurrection. Some from prior to and some after the resurrection of Jesus: Elijah raising the son of the widow of Zarephath (1 Ki. 17:17-24), Elisha raising the son of the Shunamite woman (2 Ki. 4:18-37), an Israelite man being resurrected after his body touches Elisha's bones (2 Ki. 13:20–21), Jesus compassionately raising the son of the widow in Nain (Lk. 7:11–17), the daughter of Jairus (Lk. 8:49–56), and Lazarus (Jn. 11:1-44), Jesus' own resurrection (Mt. 28:1-20), Peter raising Tabitha (Acts 9:36-42) and Paul reviving Eutychus (Acts 20:7–12). The act of resurrecting the dead is work that can only be done through relationship with God. When we allow God to use us, amazing things can happen—even the decolonizing of our faith history.

---

[297] Willie James Jennings, *The Christian Imagination: Theology and the Origins of Race* (New Haven, CT: Yale University Press, 2010), 60.

This work is active, practical, purposeful. It is what we refer to within Gospel Haymanot as "Ujamaa"—Practical Theology—faith in action. The word itself comes from a Swahili word that means 'brotherhood,' and is related to another word 'jamaa' with means 'relatives.' Ujamaa is defined in the African-American modern tradition launched in the mid-1960s as the fourth principle of Kwanzaa to mean cooperative economics and all that concept encompasses. However, a few years earlier, that term was expanded by Tanzania's first President, Julius Nyerere, to encompass "familyhood" and the understanding that people should build for themselves communally, pulling on and pooling the strengths of the people.

> We, in Africa, have no more need of being 'converted' to socialism than we have of being 'taught' democracy. Both are rooted in our own past–in the traditional society which produced us… It was in the struggle to break the grip of colonialism that we learnt the need for unity. We came to recognize that the same socialist attitude of mind which, in the tribal days, gave to every individual the security that comes of belonging to a widely extended family, must be preserved within the still wider society of the nation. But we should not stop there. Our recognition of the family to which we all belong must be extended yet further—beyond the tribe, the community, the nation, or even the continent—to embrace the whole society of mankind.[298]

The word is both a defined word and a concept. As a concept, it seems to incorporate more than the ascribed conceptualizations because there is so much more to something that is "collective" and that is "community." While all communities have boundaries of some kind, those boundaries are semi-permeable, allowing the community

---

[298] Julius K. Nyerere, *Ujamma – The Basis of African Socialism* reprinted in *The Journal of Pan African Studies* 1.1 (Los Angeles, CA: California Institute of Pan African Studies, 1987), 10-11.

to interact with its environment and neighboring communities and to change over time—hopefully for the better. Community involves movement and action. That is why we call our practical theology arm of the Society Gospel Haymanot "Ujamaa."

The work I do, teaching, faith-based counseling, and spiritual direction, is Ujamaa. It is designed to facilitate understanding, healing and a reconnection or deeper connection with God for others. The research I do is Ujamaa. It is designed to uncover lived experiences of different aspects of our faith contexts to make explicit some of the implicit processes that help us to choose life (Deut. 30:19) and have it to the full (Jn. 10:10). Understanding our better options and practices enables us to make healthier life choices, which in turn benefits community. My interest in historical trauma is Ujamaa. If there are damaging residues that dim the light in us, we need to understand the nuanced ways those residues create the shadows and recognize what we can do to counter them. Addressing historical traumas in current contexts is both individual and community level work and one can fluidly shift the work between them to facilitate restoration of the individual and the community. I will now provide some commentary from various aspects of my Ujamaa.

## The Pastor's Words

The project I call "The Pastor's Words" was a qualitative project designed to identify African-American clergy perspectives regarding intimate partner violence. The reason for this is that religious fundamentalists are more likely to go to clergy before other professional mental health providers. African-Americans seem to prefer faith-based organizations to address mental health issues and clergy are change agents regarding mental health and social interaction in African-American communities.[299] I tend to define African-American broadly

---

[299] R. J. Taylor, C. G. Ellison, L. M. Chatters, J. S. Levin, and K. D. Lincoln, *Mental Health Services in Faith Communities: The Role of Clergy in Black Churches*, Vol. 1 (Thousand Oaks, CA: Sage Publishing, Social Work, 2000), 45.

because though a person may look phenotypically African-American, that person may have hailed from another part of the world, such as the Caribbean or continental Africa and but now, at a given point in time, fully identifies as African-American. This was the case for some of my participants.

The project had two goals. One, as previously stated, to increase understanding of African-American clergy perspective of intimate partner violence (IPV) and to explore concerns regarding collaboration with community agents. Why did I study IPV? The Centers for Disease Prevention and Control identifies IPV as a public health issue that is preventable.[300] The clergy had a similar understanding of what intimate partner violence is and they knew how to define it. The clergy definition of IPV was very similar to that of the CDC and that definition is one person's abusive use of power to control another.[301] The behaviors that they identified with intimate partner violence is also similar to what was defined with the CDC, and that is physical, sexual, mental or emotional violence and threatening or intimidating behavior. However, several clergy expanded the definition of intimate partner violence by including adultery as abusive control,[302] which I believe is a unique finding in relation to clergy perspectives. Related to this was the realization that some of the participants would advocate for either separation or divorce, and that at least one of the clergy

---

[300] P. H. Niolon, M. Kearns, J. Dills, K. Rambo, S. Irving, T. Armstead, and L. Gilbert, *Preventing Intimate Partner Violence Across the Lifespan: A Technical Package of Programs, Policies, and Practices* (Atlanta, GA: National Center for Injury Prevention and Control, Centers for Disease Control and Prevention, 2017).

[301] M. J. Breiding, K. C. Basile, S. G. Smith, M. C. Black, R. R. Mahendra, *Intimate Partner Violence Surveillance: Uniform Definitions and Recommended Data Elements, Version 2.0.* (Atlanta, GA: National Center for Injury Prevention and Control, Centers for Disease Control and Prevention, 2015); T. B. Bent-Goodley, and D. N. Fowler, *Spiritual and religious abuse: Expanding what is known about domestic violence* (Thousand Oaks, CA: Sage Publishing, Affilia 2006, 21), 282.

[302] J. Dyer, "Challenging Assumptions: Clergy Perspectives and Practices Regarding Intimate Partner Violence," in *Journal of Religion & Spirituality in Social Work*, 29 (2010): 33-48.

considered serial adultery grounds for divorce, because it was a breaking of the covenant relationship.

The clergy in this study did not feel as if their training prepared them to address issues like intimate partner violence. Unfortunately, this is not an unusual finding, and clergy do lament the ways in which their training does not give them a better grasp on the intricate complications that can emerge in human relationships.[303] This information can be used to help improve the ways in which clergy are trained for their roles. Clergy participants were asked what they believed was happening with the couples that enabled intimate partner violence to manifest in their relationship and I found that in those couples, there was a downplaying of religion.

One of the most important set of findings was that the practices used by the clergy to address intimate partner violence in their churches mimicked clinical best practices. The practices identified beginning where the client is, not rushing the recovery process to give the person time to cope with trauma, prioritizing interventions, case management, advocacy, reality testing, and referrals to community providers. Though imperfectly implemented, the elements were present. What makes the use of these practices imperfect was that they tended to be distributed across several clergy instead of all being implemented by the same pastor. This kind of information counters some of the assumptions frequently made against clergy that they don't take care of the victim in a just manner. The pastors also discussed how the African-American Church culture responds to anything outside of the expected realm of Christian behavior to be somehow distasteful. The church dynamic trends toward sanitizing the Church, to use the word of one of the pastors. In some cases that means silencing those who disclosed the abuse. As we find in the broader population, there are

---

[303] J. Dyer, "Just Social Work? Collaborating with African American Clergy to Address Intimate Partner Violence in Churches," in *Journal of the North American Association of Christians in Social Work,* 46.4 (2016): 33-54.

intentional and subtle efforts to silence anyone who would spoil the image of what a Christian relationship should be. One of the most important sets of findings were the practices used by the clergy to address IPV in their churches. I was able to identify recommendations for clergy about what they do to address IPV in their churches, one of which was to address it from their pulpits directly and clearly.

The project also explored issues of what can hinder effective collaboration between African-American churches and secular community agencies. Some interesting concerns emerged. Those include that the clergy discussed a sense of feeling dismissed by some of the people who were actually trying to partner with them. This may have come from pastors feeling as if the community agencies are members of the community agencies or, in some ways, making judgments about the ways that they might be dealing with IPV and so they weren't quite received in ways that felt welcoming. There was also a concern that if the clergy referred someone that that person might not get the kinds of recommended interventions that would align with the faith practice of the particular pastor or faith. And as a result, there was reticence for making some referrals, because of a concern that the faith of the church member might not be supported by the provider. Moreover, clergy noted that some secular community agencies would state their desire to work with churches when there was a crisis of some sort or if the agency had a previously defined project. In these cases, there was usually no previous engagement with the church towards including them in the planning and no on-going relationship developed in a way that was actually just and equitable. The clergy wanted community agencies to continue to reach out to them, but just to not reach out in ways that perpetuated their concerns.

## Faith, Conflict & African-American Couples

Another project explored faith and conflict in African-American couples. This project delved into the ways that Christian couples use their faith to address conflict, wherein lies the significance of this study. Studies prior to my project were structured primarily to explore themes of what was not working in the relationship. This project investigated how something positive in the lives of the partners—their faith—was used to help keep the relationship strong and healthy. When looking at Christian relationships a few theorists might suggest that a kind of marital triad develops within the relationship.[304] The triad is created when God is incorporated into the couple interaction as a third person. I sought an increased understanding of the potential marital triad, to see how it manifested, and even if it did manifest with the couples that participated in this project.

When couples cannot resolve their conflicts, there is a greater likelihood for other maladaptive and negative behaviors to encroach into the relationship. The importance of this emerges when the partners in the couple are distressed or are in distress on a regular basis, they will have more difficulty resolving their conflicts. African-Americans exist in a high stress context due to existing in a negatively racialized environment, and research shows that African-Americans report poorer marriage quality. However, religion can mitigate both tension and distress, and African-American couples tend to be more religious.[305] I found a kind of marital math within the couples in this study: the triad. The way that they incorporated God into their relationship created the mathematics to be one plus one equals three because of God being the third member in the relationship implicitly.

All of the partners in the study noted the importance of their faith in their daily lives: through their faith they develop a sacred quality in their relationship, and it showed up in different ways. One of the ways was play. They would find healthy unexpected ways that they could

---

[304] M. H. Butler, and M. Harper, "The Divine Triangle: God in the Marital System of Religious Couples," in *Family Process* 33 (1994), 277-286.

[305] E. Brown, T. Orbuch, and J. Bauermeister, "Religiosity and Marital Stability Among Black American and White American Couples," in *Family Relations* 157 (2008), 186–197.

interact together that permitted laughter and ultimately reduction and attention. They also used silence as a means of dispersing tension, rather than to prolong or exacerbate it. They actually used it to bring down the tensions. Each would go to their own corners and allow themselves to come and once they were in a better space they would re-engage to address the issue. They incorporated God into their problem solving to resolve issues. If there was a concern from one partner about the other, the concerned partner would petition in prayer and ask God to intervene in the situation and with the other partner. This finding increased understanding of the ways that the couples incorporated God in their relationship.

Though partners in this project verbally stated race/ethnicity wasn't an issue in their marriages, when they were given a scale that measured the ethno-racial stress they experienced,[306] all but one fourth scored moderate to high on cultural stress. This speaks to the unrecognized damage that racism can cause. The stress baseline of African-Americans is very high because they have learned to live with the stress of racism. However, just like a runny nose, failure to notice it doesn't mean it's not creating a mess. The benefit of this knowledge is that service providers working with African-American couples can now appropriately enhance their work in order to address two issues: 1.) They should be sure to factor in the traumas of racism as having an unseen impact on the tensions in the relationship: 2.) Providers should also make note of the importance of faith for the couple and intentionally use interventions that incorporate their faith to strengthen the relationship.

---

[306] S. Utsey, "Development and validation of a short form of the Index of Race-Related Stress (IRRS)-brief version," in *Measurement and Evaluation in Counseling and Development* 32, 149-167 (1999), 149.

## African-American Clergy and Compassion Fatigue

The last example of the sacred work of Ujamaa is a qualitative research project that investigated the lived experiences of African-American clergy in relation to their job stress and clergy compassion fatigue. It tends to be smaller than quantitative research where you're going to get big percentages and something applicable to everyone. With qualitative research, the researcher can explore lived experience, doing deep dives into the particular phenomenon being investigated. Themes that emerge may not be applicable to everyone but may fit similar contexts. The information in my research projects emerge directly out of the African-American diaspora community. It may not be applicable to white, Latinx or Asian-American communities. However, some findings may be broadly applicable to others and some will be more reflective of the culture within the broader African-American community.

Many pastors have anecdotally discussed clergy related job-stress, likely because of the job of clergy where both pulpit & pew experience a resistance to clergy publicly talking about their issues.[307] In other words, the kinds of projections people can attribute to their leader, sometimes irrationally, do not always permit them to have their own needs. Also, transparent sharing from leaders about their struggles may sometimes negatively backfire. As a result, clergy may be reluctant to get help they may need, especially if it is mental health related, and may feel isolation due to job-related stress. Unaddressed clergy stress may trigger clergy compassion fatigue. They are talking about it with people who are friends but are not necessarily putting it out in the public sphere. There are ways that people think about the work of clergy that may create a certain resistance, both from the pulpit and

---

[307] Michael Maccoby, *Why People Follow the Leader: The Power of Transference*, (Boston, MA: Harvard Business Publishing, 2004).

the pew, to the pastor sharing the pastor's struggles in a public space. This can complicate clergy's ability and willingness to get the support they may need.

In this study with clergy, I found that the men started earlier in ministry and had longer and more uninterrupted ministry careers. The women started their careers at later stages of their life and experienced much less support than the man. These are not surprising findings. The men tended to be married and fewer of the women were married. The men were mentored more than twice that type of support for the women. In personal and professional contexts, there is a question of accessibility of support for the women in their most immediate social spaces. Most of the participants felt as if they were not trained to address the difficulties of ministry. The importance of this kind of study is that of understanding the impact of compassion fatigue on people who lead notable segments of the African-American community. These are leaders in the Church, which is a fairly significant portion of the African-American community at this stage. It is a state of being that might impact their ability to stay connected in healthy ways to communities they lead.

Some of the underlying stress is race related, because that is unavoidable if you are Black and Brown in this country. Added to that are the stresses of having to do a job with ambiguous boundaries and role overload, that you realize your training did not fully prepare you to do. If the leader is unhealthy, the dysfunctions can seep into the community being led, and this can have detrimental consequences. However, being aware of the needs of this population, will facilitate the ways in which community providers can support them, not just in relation to the multiple stressors they experience on the job, but also, by recognizing and factoring in the traumas that can be building in the background due to ethno-racial stresses.

It is so important as we think about different ways that practical theology—Ujamaa—is implemented and how it's utilized, not to neglect the contributions of social science research and how it contributes to the upbuilding of God's Kingdom. For me, and the research that I do, it is about bringing information into the community in ways that can benefit and change certain dynamics that are not healthy. My work is just the tip of the iceberg in relation to the full manifestation of work practical theologians can develop that can benefit the people within our Christian African diaspora community.

Ujamaa effectively clears a path to God as we identify and address the noise that can get in the way and prevent people being healthy, seeing God, and having a vibrant relationship with God. The work that we are doing, Ujamaa, can facilitate change and open up understanding. We are among those who are calling out to make straight, a way in the desert (Jn. 1:23). This is indeed sacred work. Though all are one body, God will use each of us for different purposes, just like the parts of the body having different functions (1 Cor. 12:12-27). We are called to this work, and as we do it through God, Who is our Enabler, we help to create better lives among those in the Kingdom.

Thank you for permitting me the honor and pleasure of sharing with you how excited I am about what God is doing. I know that as we continue to work, each one of us does amazing Kingdom work with the part of the puzzle God wants us to put into place. For those who are called to this function of practical theology, and who take on not only the work of Gospel Haymanot but the particular mantle of Ujamaa, we do sacred work.

# The Principle of Subsidiarity and John M. Perkins' Model of Christian Community Development

## RaShan A. Frost

Social institutions must have a cooperative relationship in order to produce a healthy society. The way in which these roles are exercised in harmony with one another either facilitates or inhibits the pursuit of the common good. Therefore, determining the scope of involvement between the larger and smaller social institutions determines their level of responsibility. In light of this, how does the state interact with institutions such as the individual, the family, and the church for the good of society? One way to answer this question is by examining how Christian political theology, specifically, Catholic social teaching addresses the responsibility of social institutions in the pursuit of human flourishing.

The principle of subsidiarity is a Catholic social teaching that calls for esteeming the full richness of social life through ordering the contributions that come from various societal associations, ranging from the family unit to the government.[308] The overall

---

[308] U.S. Catholic Bishops, "Economic Justice For All: A Pastoral Letter on Catholic Social Teaching and the U. S. Economy" in *Catholic Social Thought: The Documentary Heritage*, Expanded Edition, ed. David J. O'Brien and Thomas A. Shannon (Maryknoll, NY: Orbis, 2010), 721.

premise of subsidiarity is that "nothing should be done by a larger and more complex organization which can be done well by a smaller and simpler organization."[309] This principle seeks to decentralize activity to the most basic, fundamental and localized societal structure possible.

This paper seeks to address how the principle of subsidiarity can be applied within a Protestant ministry context, particularly, John M. Perkins' work in community development.[310] Perkins established a "3 R" strategy of Christian Community Development (CCD)—relocation, reconciliation, and redistribution—as a means of addressing issues of poverty and seeking the common good within the urban context of the United States.[311]

In order to combat the issue of poverty, Perkins contends that successful community development must be contextualized at the local level.[312] Perkins' belief of a localized emphasis of community development is comparable to the idea of subsidiarity although he does not

---

[309] David A. Bosnich, "The Principle of Subsidiarity," *Religion & Liberty* 6.4, July 20, 2010, https://acton.org/pub/religion-liberty/volume-6-number-4/principle-subsidiarity.

[310] John M. Perkins is a minister, activist, and public theologian who was the founder of the Christian Community development Association. He is also the President Emeritus of the John and Vera Mae Perkins Foundation for Justice, Reconciliation, and Community Development. Perkins' ministry focuses on how to engage the local community and the poor from a wholistic approach from a biblical worldview. He developed this strategy while doing ministry in his home state of Mississippi during the Civil Rights Movement and later in California. For a more detailed account of the life of John M. Perkins and how he developed his ministry, refer to his autobiography, *Let Justice Roll Down*: John M. Perkins, *Let Justice Roll Down* (Grand Rapids, MI: Baker Books, 1976). For a more detailed examination of his 3R strategy for Christian Community Development, see *With Justice For All:* John Perkins, *With Justice For All: A Strategy for Community Development*, Revised and Updated (Grand Rapids, MI: Baker Books, 2014).

[311] The Christian Community Development Association has expanded Perkins' 3 R strategy to eight key components: redistribution, relocation, reconciliation, leadership development, empowerment, wholistic approach, church-based, and listening to the community. Christian Community Development Association. "CCD Philosophy," accessed May 27, 2021. https://ccda.org/about/philosophy/.

[312] John M. Perkins, *Beyond Charity: The Call to Christian Community Development* (Grand Rapids, MI: Baker Books, 1993), 90.

attribute his strategy to this principle. I argue that the principle of subsidiarity provides a viable means of examining John M. Perkins' view of CCD, specifically the aspect of redistribution. First, I will provide a brief overview of the principle of subsidiarity and Perkins' strategy of CCD. Finally, I will articulate how the principle of subsidiarity can be synthesized with Perkins' view of redistribution regarding the role of the family and the local church.

## The Principle of Subsidiarity

The foundations of the principle of subsidiarity is found in Leo XIII's 1891 encyclical, *Rerum Novarum*. In it, Leo addresses the rise of socialism and the Industrial Revolution, which together, created a tension between the civil and ecclesiastical authorities and how they interacted with other aspects of social life.[313] Leo advocates for a line of demarcation between the state and the family, noting that the state should protect the sovereignty of both the individual and the family: "The State must not absorb the individual or the family; both should be allowed free and untrammeled action as far as it is consistent with the common good and the interests of others."[314] Furthermore, the state has the responsibility not to "absorb the individual or the family," but to also "safeguard the community and all its parts."[315] The responsibility of safeguarding the integrity and autonomy of the individual and the family resides with the state, and the state should honor that responsibility.

*Rerum Novarum* also argues that the state has an obligation to avoid "undue interference" and that safeguards are necessary to

---

[313] David J. O'Brien and Thomas A. Shannon, ed. *Catholic Social Thought: Encyclicals and Documents from Pope Leo XIII to Pope Francis*, 3rd ed. (Maryknoll, NY: Orbis, 2016), 13.
[314] Leo XIII, "Rerum Novarum" in *Catholic Social Thought: Encyclicals and Documents form Pope Leo XIII to Pope Francis*, 3rd ed., ed. David J. O'Brien and Thomas A. Shannon (Maryknoll, NY: Orbis, 2010), 28.
[315] Leo XIII, "Rerum Novarum," 28.

prevent unwanted intervention.[316] The ideas in *Rerum Novarum* would be further developed and articulated as the principle of subsidiarity in subsequent encyclicals. Forty years after *Rerum Novarum*, Pius XI established the parameters for the relationship between the various social institutions and introduced the term subsidiarity in *Quadragesimo Anno:*

> The State authorities should leave to other bodies the care of expediting of business and activities of lesser moment, which otherwise become for it a source of great distraction....Let those in power, therefore, be convinced that the more faithfully this principle of "subsidiarity" is followed and a hierarchical order prevails among the various organizations, the more excellent will be the authority and efficiency of society, and the happier and more prosperous the condition of the commonwealth.[317]

Pius argues that the principle of subsidiarity when practiced improves the overall well-being of society by allowing every social institution to operate in a manner that maximizes efficiency while respecting levels of authority. Therefore, the overall premise of subsidiarity is that the state should confer to the local social entities, the authority and ability to implement activities that will impact their specific social context.

---

[316] Leo XIII, "Rerum Novarum," 32.

[317] Pius XI, "Quadragesimo Anno," in *Catholic Social Thought: Encyclicals and Documents form Pope Leo XIII to Pope Francis*, 3rd ed., ed. David J. O'Brien and Thomas A. Shannon (Maryknoll, NY: Orbis, 2010), 80.

## John M. Perkins' 3 R Strategy for Christian Community Engagement

Perkins strategy for CCD—relocation, reconciliation, and redistribution—was developed for the purpose of pursuing the common good by implementing justice for the poor as expressed through the gospel.[318] He defines justice as an economic issue regarding the stewardship of God's resources in a way that is available to all people.[319] When people do not have the access to opportunities that can lead to flourishing, injustice becomes the inevitable outcome.

For Perkins, the primary mediating institution that facilitates the pursuit of justice and the public good is the local church. The social location of the church must be situated among the poor and desolate as a prophetic witness that proclaims the totality of the gospel and addresses the needs of the whole person.[320] Because the gospel speaks to all aspects of human life, the church's work toward justice and the common good is wholistic—addressing the spiritual, physical, economic, and political aspects of the community.

Relocation is where believers seek the good of the community by becoming neighbors who enter into the needs of that particular community. Perkins says, "[s]hared needs and friendships become a bridge for communicating the good news of Jesus Christ and working together for better conditions in the community."[321] Therefore, relocation allows for the church to take a posture of identifying with the needs of the community

---

[318] In discussing how justice pursues the common good Perkins says: "We work for justice by helping the poor to know and understand this good God of creation, by assisting them in finding opportunities to work with their own hands, by affirming their dignity and worth, and by them then being able to raise their hands in praise of this good God, our Provider," John M. Perkins, "The Christian and Biblical Justice," in *Transforming Our World: A Call to Action*, ed. James Montgomery Boice (Portland, OR: Multnomah, 1988), 108–09.

[319] Perkins, *Beyond Charity*, 127.

[320] Peter Slade, Charles Marsh, and Peter Goodwin Heltzel, *Mobilizing for the Common Good: The Lived Theology of John M. Perkins* (Jackson, MS: University Press of Mississippi, 2013), 117.

[321] Slade, Marsh and Heltzel, *Mobilizing for the Common Good*, 110–11.

because they are a part of the community thus having a vested interest in seeking its good. Relocation from a CCD perspective recognizes that when people relocate into a neighborhood, it is imperative that people take a vested interest in their community because it is now their home and they are actively participating within the indigenous culture.[322]

Reconciliation communicates the heart of gospel, restoring the broken relationships of humanity back to God and each other. Perkins points to the gospel's reconciliatory purpose: "[t]he purpose of the gospel is to bring reconciliation across racial, cultural, and economic barriers and to make people followers of Christ."[323] The church, therefore, is to be God's agents of reconciliation by bringing people into a right relationship with God through Christ and building bridges that overcome the dividing lines of society. Perkins argues that this work is done through evangelism, economic development, and social action, and that the church is responsible for making sure these duties are carried out.[324]

Finally, redistribution is the political and economic component of his strategy. Perkins argues that the fundamental flaw of free enterprise is human greed and that its implications lead to profit at the expense of exploiting others.[325] Therefore, redistribution is about understanding the idea of wealth in terms of having the proper outlook of resource ownership.[326] In other words, wealth is about first understanding that everything

---

[322] It is worth noting here that Perkins is not talking about a Christianized form of gentrification. When one relocates into a community, they are to respect the culture of that community by participating within it, not trying to change it by imposing an outside culture into it.

[323] Slade, Marsh and Heltzel, *Mobilizing for the Common Good*, 112.

[324] For more information about the work of the church in CCD, see: John Perkins, *A Quiet Revolution: The Christian Response to Human Need...A Strategy for Today* (Waco, TX: Word Books, 1976).

[325] John M. Perkins, *With Justice for All: A Strategy for Community Development* (Grand Rapids, MI: Baker, 2011), 179.

[326] Perkins expounds: "A truly Christian economic system would begin with the fact that the earth is the Lord's, not ours, and that God and God alone has the authority to determine how his wealth will be used. Our job as stewards is to carry out His will. A Christian economic system would recognize that God provides the earth's resources for all mankind, not just for some," Perkins, *With Justice for All*, 179.

belongs to God, and people have a responsibility to steward it in a way that benefits all people. It is important to note that Perkins is not advocating for socialism, or solely a state mandated redistribution of wealth, but rather a voluntary communal redistribution of resources, including wealth, thereby maximizing the economic flourishing. While income is a key aspect of Perkins' view of redistribution, his emphasis is on economic opportunity.[327] Perkins believes that poor communities suffer due to the lack of the economic, educational, and political opportunities that promotes flourishing. Redistribution, therefore, entails not only the sharing of economic resources but also the skills, technology, and educational resources that empowers people to break out of the cycle of poverty and maximize their agency in society for the common good.[328]

## Applying the Principle of Subsidiarity to Perkins' View of Redistribution

CCD is a social and economic endeavor that incorporates all of the various institutions of social life. For Perkins, the idea of upward economic mobility for an individual or a group does not occur in a vacuum, but rather with a resource input that facilitates mobility. In light of this, the resource input needed to break the cycle of poverty needs to originate from within the community.[329] Perkins argues that local institutions should have the greatest bearing of influence in

---

[327] Wayne Gordon and John M. Perkins, *Making Neighborhoods Whole: A Handbook for Christian Community Development* (Downers Grove, IL: IVP Books, 2013), 76. Perkins continues: "But everyone ought to have a fair opportunity for the good things in life, and the plain truth is that in our culture and cultures around the world they do not. The playing field is not level. Regardless of the society, those in control tend to make laws and establish policies that consider their own interests over the interests of others—especially the poor, who are often voiceless and disenfranchised," 77.

[328] Perkins, *Beyond Charity*, 37.

[329] Perkins, *Let Justice Roll Down*, 122. Perkins says: "the community itself must develop its potential to utilize and multiply economic resources. When programs are designed by the helpers, the helpees (sic) (to coin a term) don't always get much help," Perkins, *Let Justice Roll Down*, 122.

developing the community: "In order to combat the cycle of discouragement, ignorance and exploitation, it seems to me that there is a basic need for indigenous organizations and communities whose life substance feeds on local efforts, local training and local leadership."[330]

Perkins also argues that oftentimes the assistance of the state, while well intentioned, actually perpetuates the cycle of poverty: "[c]entral to the failure of the welfare system is the fact that it tried to fix a fixed 'solution' on all the nation's poor, doing very little to answer specific concrete needs at the local level."[331] The issue that Perkins has with federal intervention is its inability to contextualize the assistance to meet the needs of the local community. He advocates for a 'bottom up' approach, meaning that the programs and services that are designed to benefit a local community reflect the actual needs of the people being served.[332] The most effective way to assist and empower the local community must come from the community itself, ensuring that the actual needs of that specific community will be met through the most effective means possible.

Subsidiarity affirms the necessity of community ownership of creating avenues of flourishing, and articulates the dangers of the state providing the primary means of social assistance.[333] When the

---

[330] Perkins, *Let Justice Roll Down*, 121.

[331] Perkins, *Beyond Charity*, 103.

[332] Perkins, *Beyond Charity*, 103. A Catholic position of this can be found in John XIII encyclical *Mater Et Magistra*: "Those who rely on their own resources and initiative should contribute as best they can to the equitable adjustment of economic life in their community," John XIII, *Mater Et Magistra: Christianity and Social Progress,* in *Catholic Social Thought: Encyclicals and Documents form Pope Leo XIII to Pope Francis*, 3rd ed., ed., David J. O'Brien and Thomas A. Shannon (Maryknoll, NY: Orbis, 2010), 114.

[333] John Paul II says: "By intervening directly and depriving society of its responsibility, the social assistance state leads to a loss of human energies and an inordinate increase of public agencies, which are dominated more by bureaucratic ways of thinking than by concern for serving their clients, and which are accompanied by an enormous increase in spending. In fact, it would appear that needs are best understood and satisfied by people closest to them and who act as neighbors to those in need," John Paul II, "Centesimus Annus: On the Hundredth Anniversary of Rerum Novarum," in *Catholic Social Thought: Encyclicals and Documents form Pope Leo XIII to Pope Francis*, 3rd ed., ed. David J. O'Brien and Thomas A. Shannon (Maryknoll, NY: Orbis, 2010), 512.

state becomes the primary agent for local community assistance, it oftentimes fails to provide specific and contextual solutions to meet the needs of the community leading to problems administering resources. Additionally, the state ends up creating a self-perpetuating system that never alleviates community ills. Perkins recognized this to be the primary problem of government led assistance programs. Government programs oftentimes treated symptoms without addressing the underlying social and economic problems and as a result, produced little incentive to fix the real problem.[334] Redistribution, within the context of subsidiarity, seeks to foster a sense of empowerment and responsibility of those in the community, thus creating environments that affirm human dignity amongst the poor and marginalized. In Kansas City's east side, local churches with the support of local business and civic leaders, a Christian-centered gathering space called the Hope Center was created. Out of that came the Hope Leadership Academy and the Hope Family Care Center. These institutions provided educational assistance, college preparation, job skill training, and medical care.[335] Additionally, redistribution emphasizes economic development through microenterprise as a way to help entrepreneurs start businesses within the community in order to meet the needs of the community and improve its economy.[336]

For Perkins, economic development begins with developing people through education, leadership development, and economic empowerment, thus empowering people to fully recognize their dignity and actualize their potential as human beings. Because of this, the state should not interfere in the "internal life of a community of lower order," in order not to deprive the local community their ownership

---

[334] Perkins, *With Justice for All*, 171.
[335] Tom Nelson, *The Economics of Neighborly Love*, (Downers Grove, IL: IVP), 2017.
[336] Gordon and Perkins, *Making Neighborhoods Whole*, 79.

of the systems and structures that facilitate their own flourishing.[337] Therefore, whatever function the state has should be one of a cooperative capacity, providing support for local institutions in areas that they cannot adequately perform or resource on their own.

## The Family

The family is the foundational unit of society and is the lifeblood of the community. It is worth noting that, for Perkins, the idea of the family as the foundational unit of society derives from the biblical understanding that the family consisting of a biological man and woman married to one another and having children. While the extended family, members such as grandparents, aunts, uncles, and cousins are not excluded, the most foundational suit of society is a man and woman united in marriage and having children. Healthy individuals and communities are linked to the health of marriages and families. Perkins argues that when societies break down, it usually stems from the breakdown of the family:

> The problems of my community are the problems of America….and I can tell you that the issue we're facing is the broken family and the broken community….The community is broken because families are broken, and families can't get back together because the community is broken. This is why

---

[337] John Paul II, "Centesimus Annus," 512. John Paul II elaborates: "Economic activity… cannot be conducted in an institutional, juridical or political vacuum. On the contrary, it presupposes sure guarantees of individual freedom…and efficient public services. Hence the principal task of the state is to guarantee this security, so that those who work and produce can enjoy the fruits of their labors and thus feel encouraged to work efficiently and honestly.… Another task of the state is that of overseeing and directing the exercise of human rights in the economic sector. However, primary responsibility in this area belongs not to the state but to individuals and to the various groups and associations which makes up society…the state has a duty to sustain business activities by creating conditions which will ensure job opportunities, by stimulating those activities where they are lacking or by supporting them in moments of crisis," John Paul II, "Centesimus Annus," 511–12.

family values and social justice aren't separate issues. The health of the community depends on the health of the family and the health of the family depends on the justice of the community.[338]

Perkins is making the case that when families are broken, the community at large suffers. In other words, the health of the community is directly related to the health of the family. If this is the case as Perkins proposes, then what role does the state play if families or individuals are unable or unwilling to assume familial and societal responsibilities? Because the family is the foundation of society, all social organizations should work toward the welfare of the family.[339] For Perkins, redistribution is about economically empowering the family in order to empower the community.[340] Because the family is the most fundamental institution of society, CCD strives to provide localized assistance meeting specific needs and Perkins argues that the local church is the institution that can best fulfill this role due to its overall mission and proximity to the family.

## The Church

If the family is the foundational unit of society, then the church is its moral anchor. The religious mission of the church is to provide "a light, and an energy which can serve to structure and consolidate the human community according to the divine law."[341] The gospel provides the theological and moral DNA for the church to be engaged

---

[338] Charles Marsh and John M. Perkins, *Welcoming Justice: God's Movement Toward Beloved Community*, 2nd ed. (Downers Grove, IL: IVP Books, 2018), 113; see also, Perkins, "The Christian and Biblical Justice," 111.
[339] Second Vatican Council, "Gaudium Et Spes," in *Catholic Social Thought: Encyclicals and Documents from Pope Leo XIII to Pope Francis,* 3rd ed., ed. David J. O'Brien and Thomas A. Shannon, (Maryknoll, NY: Orbis, 2016), 210–11.
[340] Marsh and Perkins, *Welcoming Justice*, 114.
[341] Marsh and Perkins, *Welcoming Justice*, 200–201.

in the local community. For Perkins, this religious mission extends into the economic and political life of the local community.[342] CCD grows from and is dependent upon the active presence of the local church within its context.

Perkins' ecclesiology is centered on the role of the church as a family. Due to the breakdown of the biological family, Perkins sees the church as the "true instantiation of family"—a contextualized body that is able to redeem the distorted practices of the family with the gospel.[343] This localized body is the heart of CCD, connected in worship and mobilized for service and rebuilding community. Perkins argues that this mobilization is only possible when the church operates under the parish concept as a localized family of faith.[344] The parish concept is defined by the local church caring for its parishioners and loving and serving those within its parish, the neighborhood or community the church is located. The parish concept provides an opportunity for the local church to become a community where people can find support from birth to adulthood.

Furthermore, the church is not limited to activities identified with Christian piety. The church is the community of God's people situated within a particular social location. Therefore, it is the Church's responsibility to love and serve their neighbors and to seek the common good of the neighborhood in which they reside. This responsibility and activity, however, is not in isolation to other local institutions. The local church collaborates with other homegrown institutions while providing the moral authority and spiritual direction for other

---

[342] Perkins has a diagram outlining the roles of the church. With the church at the center of the circle, there are words intersecting the circle: "the call," "evangelism," "social action," "economic development," and "justice," John M. Perkins, *A Quiet Revolution: The Christian Response to Human Need, a Strategy for Today* (Waco, TX: Word Books, 1976), 13.

[343] Slade, Marsh, and Heltzel, *Mobilizing for the Common Good*, 21.

[344] John M. Perkins, *Restoring At-Risk Communities: Doing It Together and Doing It Right* (Grand Rapids, MI: Baker Books, 1996), 173.

institutions as they serve the community.[345] The collaborative function of the church is not limited to faith-based non-profit organizations and para-church ministries but also local businesses for the purposes of economic development.[346] In the spirit of subsidiarity, the role of the church serves as the mediator between other social institutions, facilitating cooperation and development in ways that the federal government cannot due to the localization of the church as a vital part of community life. The local church in cooperation with other community entities ought to be a catalytic agent for economic intervention and political action, thus being able to affect change at the level where it is most needed in a way that is most effective.

## Conclusion

CCD working within the framework of subsidiarity points to the necessity of indigenous social institutions having ownership over their own flourishing by being the primary facilitator of localized social and economic action. While Perkins recognizes the necessity of the federal government in alleviating poverty, he understands that their role must be limited so that people can have ownership over their

---

[345] Gordon and Perkins, *Making Neighborhoods Whole*, 122-125. CCD claims that this moral authority and spiritual direction is primarily directed towards para-church ministries and faith-based non-profits.

[346] Perkins says: "Churches can support these businesses by using their services. The American church is a wealthy institution; I think it is very appropriate for churches to use their wealth in ways that will bring about economic development....Churches can also help businesses raise capital that might not be available from a bank. Many churches invest large amounts of money. Why not invest it in businesses that are part of community development?" Perkins, *Beyond Charity*, 123. Perkins also talks about the importance of starting local enterprises and cooperatives for the purposes of economic development. He says: "Ministries in the CCDA are attempting to change disparity between the haves and the have-nots through supporting microenterprise—helping entrepreneurs start businesses that not only meet the needs of the community but that also improve the economy of the community. This happens when businesses are based in the community; money made by those businesses is recycled within the community as opposed to exiting to some other place." Gordon and Perkins, *Making Neighborhoods Whole*, 79.

own flourishing.[347] His model shows how redistribution provides a system of cooperative social responsibility with the local institutions being the primary agent for community development while the federal government provides support. He does not negate the role of the state in this endeavor, but situates their responsibility in a support capacity. This paper introduces the principle of subsidiarity in connection to Perkin's principle of redistribution. For Perkins, the family and the local church are key to redistribution because the skills, talents, and resources of these institutions are what is used to meet the needs of the community. Until there is a development and redistribution of human resources, material resources will be limited. The scope of this paper is limited; it did not go into detail regarding other institutions, like business. Although this paper precludes a more detailed examination of Perkins's strategy of redistribution, the reader is introduced to the idea of how the principle of subsidiarity can be examined and applied within models of CCD.

---

[347] Perkins says: "Working with officials takes away the attitude that government should do everything for us. I believe that government should make it possible for us to do things for ourselves...If we can take responsibility to carry out our own dreams, we have a greater sense of ownership and more pride in the results," Perkins, *Beyond Charity*, 106.

# Book Reviews

*After Whiteness: An Education in Belonging*, Willie James Jennings, William B. Eerdmans Publishing Co. (ISBN: 978-0-8028-7844-1), 174 pp., $19.99 (paper)

The brilliant Willie James Jennings has published the opening volume in Eerdmans' "Theological Education between the Times" series. *After Whiteness* provides invaluable insight into white, Western theological academia as reflected by Dr. Jennings' distinguished career that is seasoned all throughout with stories and poetry that erotically illustrate the book's vision for belonging in (white) theological academia beyond whiteness.

Jennings powerfully illustrates the oppression that Black and other scholars of color must bear when we "too quickly imagine that the…voices I heard through texts matched authors who would see me, a black man, as their conversation partner," (p. 2). These and other embodied traumas that Black scholars bear in white academia set the state for many of the "secrets" that Jennings elucidates in the preface of the work. "Escape" is the first secret—theological education as escape from racial and socio-economic oppression. "Formation" is held up as the central theme of the book. Western education and theological education have been plagued by a distorted formation that centers the white self-sufficient man as the captivating model for educational formation (pp. 6-7). The definition of "whiteness" is taken out of its common understanding as reference to European descent and refers to a seductive way of being that leads to hegemony (p. 9). Perhaps of greatest interest to this present journal and academic society, Jennings then turns to address scholars of color who seek to reject Western hegemonic forms of education and build academic spaces committed to communities of color: "That skepticism, founded at the opening moments of colonial conquest, yet grows and fosters a quiet despair that moves through the educational ecologies of theological schools," (p. 10). I agree with the brother that we belong to each other. All we tryin' to say is can't white folks come "belong" in institutions they don't primarily run and can't people of color center their theological interlocutions in white institutions? We don't want to be "free" of white tutelage; but the question is: why is the work of belonging always one-directional (i.e., people of color come into historically-oppressive white spaces and help them be better)? But lemme get back to the review.

The first theme Jennings explores is that of the *fragments* that have shaped white theological education in positive and negative ways: 1.) The Fragment of Faith (pp. 32-35): the slivers and shards through which humans glimpse faith and tradition, illustrated biblically by the pieces of bread distributed to the multitude (Mt. 14:19); 2.) The Fragment of Colonial Power (pp. 35-40): the cultural fragments with which people of color assemble post-colonialism and that are (lamentably) contrasted with the encounter of "Christianity" (i.e., Western Colonialism); and 3.) The Fragment of Commodification (pp. 41-44): the corporeal, terrestrial and intellectual reduction of creation and ideas to being mere possessions. The fragments of faith and culture should be leveraged to resist the fragment of commodification through new *designs* that lead to the place of communion. Chapter Two explores the theme of *designs*, initially focusing on the design of forced affection for material that has been curated through a Eurocentric gaze. Jennings conflates this apt critique of forced pedagogical affection with a concern over the trend in academia to advocate for or against theological orthodoxy (p. 65). The design of forced affection must be met with the designs of cultivating intellectual affection, discerning love that can perform exclusion in a way that invites deeper listening, and theological resistance that *builds* community (pp. 66-75).

The theme of *building* is set against the destructive image of the plantation that Jennings argues has shaped the construction of theological institutions. Theological education in the Western world has been built "inside an ecclesial reality inside a white patriarchal domesticity, shaped by an overwhelming white masculinist presence that always aims to build a national and global future that we should all inhabit," (p. 82). These forms of distorted institutionalizing practices must be replaced with life-giving institutional performance that give room for the builders of theological institutions (p. 84). Building upon the plantation imagery, Jennings characterizes the building approaches in two primary categories: those who promote the plantation-vision of effectivity or those who abide in the surface of institutions in constant resistance and suspicion. The way forward is to embrace the divinely ordained mandate to build, and to build towards life, with *motions* that move towards freedom (p. 104). The people of an institution must be built towards one another through a reframing of the daily motions of schools with renewed vision of edification (p. 105). Some of the motions that have characterized theological institutions are freedom of mastery (moral formation) and mastery of freedom (emancipation) (p. 108). Introspection—the state of being that organizes the external world through internal calculus—and introspection—the act of looking inwardly—form another "motion binary" that have been largely framed by the plantation in Western theological education that inhibit communion (p. 114). Embracing the freedom to not know (p. 120) and embracing critique (p. 129) are actions that reject a colonial, plantation-formed process of educational motions. Formation, the educational journey and critical dissent all must lead, for Jennings, to communion bound by holy *eros* (p. 134).

Educational gatherings must resist the "colonial options for knowing," which are identified as race, nationality and religion (p. 139). I agree with the second one being colonial; but the other two are biblical (Jas. 1:27; Rev. 22:16). Additionally, educational gatherings must move past the colonial effect of reducing the scholastic community to an "exchange network of modern capitalism," (p. 146). The impulse control bodies, which Jennings identifies as a function of whiteness, is a distorted *erotic* power that must be replaced with the *erotic* love that characterizes the community gathered around Jesus (p. 151). The book ends with final exhortations to envisage theological education as a community that engenders hope and points to eternity (p. 157). In sum, Jennings has produced yet another thought-provoking, intimate and poetic work of scholarship. I wish that *After Whiteness* offered direction for theological educators who work in institutions and pedagogical frameworks rooted in non-Western academic contexts, to take his beautiful vision of education out of the plantation of Western, white-dominated contexts. However, his vision of new designs, buildings and motions, utilizing the fragments of Scripture and culture in a context of eros retain multiple avenues of application, especially for an Afrocentric theological context.

Vince L. Bantu<br>
Meachum School of Haymanot<br>
Fuller Theological Seminary

*African American Readings of Paul: Reception, Resistance, and Transformation*, Lisa M. Bowens, Wm. B. Eerdmans Publishing Co. (ISBN 978-0-8028-7676-8), 355 pp., $40.00 (hardcover)

Lisa M. Bowens has performed a remarkable and invaluable service for all serious Bible readers by bringing some "hidden figures" into the light. She masterfully chronicles the history of African-American biblical interpretation as it relates to the apostle Paul (i.e., Paul's disputed as well as undisputed letters, along with Paul's voice in Acts, and even Hebrews, which was commonly taken to be a Pauline composition). While reading *African American Readings of Paul*, I was struck by how frequently Acts 17:26 gets cited by the many African-American biblical interpreters that Bowens discusses. At one point, I took a glance at the index of Bowens' well-researched and cogently argued monograph, and noted that the passage is referenced much more than any other passage. Acts 17:26, words from the Apostle Paul's mouth as recorded by Luke, prompted African-American Christians over the years to see themselves within God's grand story despite the way many white Christians distorted that story. Bowens eventually addresses explicitly what I'd been observing about the role of Paul's words in Acts, noting: "As we have seen time and again in the above analysis, Acts 17:26, in which Paul states that God has made of one blood all the nations of the earth, is the *sine qua non* for many African Americans in their understanding of who Paul is and what he believes," (p. 299). The persistent use of this verse is one example of how African-American Bible-readers, from our earliest days, challenged scriptural interpretations that devalued, dehumanized, and even demonized us. Our forebears read Paul subversively "to protest white supremacy, slavery, the slave trade, black dehumanization, and male-centered readings that prohibit women preachers," (p. 12).

After an engaging foreword by Emerson Powery, Bowens gives an introduction to "African American Pauline Hermeneutics" where she lays out her goal of providing a *Wirkungsgeschichte* (reception history) of African-American Pauline interpretation. The first three chapters of *African American Readings of Paul* are arranged chronologically, with Bowens focusing on: 1.) enslaved interpreters of the early eighteenth into the early nineteenth centuries; 2.) the stories and ministries of escapees from slavery during the mid-to-late nineteenth century; and 3.) the writings of authors of the late nineteenth to mid-twentieth centuries, who dealt with post-slavery challenges in the form of segregation and Jim Crow laws. After that, Bowens focuses on some conversion stories of various African-American Christians, then concludes her work with a chapter on "African American Pauline Hermeneutics and the Art of Biblical Interpretation" where she summarizes what comes before and also wonders "where do we go from here?" (p. 305). There is a thoughtful afterword by Beverly Gaventa, who acknowledges how early African-American exegetes were in some ways ahead of their time with their interpretations and observations of Pauline passages.

Not all of the people Bowens highlights are well-known to contemporary readers, but we are treated to the voices of both famous and obscure saints through direct quotations of their words. As if collecting the words of our African-American Christian forebears was not already a profitable and powerful undertaking, Bowens also demonstrates how the social location of these interpreters influenced their reading of Paul, just as the white majority's social location influenced their interpretations. In examining the notion of social location (i.e., all that makes up a reader's identity and life situation), Bowens uncovers what she calls the *dialectic of experience*, which she defines as bringing "their experiences as African Americans to the text while at the same time allowing the text, specifically Paul's words, to interpret their experiences. There is a dynamic interplay between black lives and the biblical text," (p. 296). While white biblical interpretation generally served to reinforce white dominance and patriarchy, many African-American interpreters asserted black humanity, dignity, and empowerment—including that of black women. Black women—in every era that Bowen discusses—ironically appealed to Paul when describing their own calls into ministry. Bowens makes the provocative claim that women interpreters "utilize their female bodies to interpret Paul," (p. 111). This observation is made with regard to the ministries of Jarena Lee and Zilpha Elaw, but is part of Bowens' larger topic she calls "body hermeneutic," where interpreters ask, "Can my black body interpret Paul, and can Paul interpret my black body?" (p. 302).

On the one hand, it comes as no surprise that any Christian—including African-Americans—should cite Paul, who is prominent as a character or author in half the New Testament (i.e., Acts and the books that bear Paul's name). On the other hand, however, we might be surprised that not all African-Americans approach Paul with a hermeneutic of suspicion. We have had good reason to be suspicious in light of Pauline "household code" passages requiring women to submit to their husbands (Eph. 5:22; Col. 3:18) and slaves to obey their masters (Eph. 6:5; Col 3:22). African-American Christians have had mixed responses to Paul's writings, ranging from what Abraham Smith calls "reverential appropriation" to outright rejection.[348] But Bowens has demonstrated that while African-American biblical interpretation is not monolithic, there has been a common thread throughout the centuries of reading Paul as a liberating voice rather than an oppressive one.

In addition to detailing the words of various biblical interpreters, Bowens also gives us more than a passing glimpse of African-American church history. One stellar example is her discussion of

---

[348] Abraham Smith, "Paul and African American Biblical Interpretation," in *True to Our Native Land: An African American New Testament Commentary*, ed. Brian K. Blount, Cain Hope Felder, Clarice J. Martin, and Emerson B. Powery (Minneapolis, MN: Fortress Press, 2007), 35-36

the Azuza Street Revival of the early twentieth century. Bowens brings us voices, which might have remained hidden, into the wider conversations concerning biblical interpretation (p. 291-92). Yet Lisa Bowens not only informs us, she embodies the very practice she discusses: she is an African-American woman who, through careful analysis and thoughtful questions, provides Bible-readers with greater insight into the Apostle Paul's legacy.

Dennis R. Edwards<br>
North Park Theological Seminary

*Reading While Black: African American Biblical Interpretation as an Exercise in Hope,* Esau McCaulley, InterVarsity Press Academic (ISBN: 978-0-8308-5486-8), 208 pp., $18.00 (paper)

*Reading While Black* addresses the lack of space for Black biblical interpretation within the world of higher theological education. By an engaging use of anecdotal vignettes from his life including his early upbringing in Huntsville, Alabama, Esau McCaulley provides the reader with a Black biblical hermeneutic that he denotes as "Black Ecclesial Interpretation." In Chapter 1, McCaulley refers to biblical interpretation that is derived "from Black scholars and pastors formed by the faith found in the foundational and ongoing doctrinal commitments, sermons, public witness, and ethos of the Black church," (p. 4). The Black Christian tradition is not monolithic but it is orthodox. The theological underpinnings of Black Christianity are the same as that of Evangelicalism (p. 5). However, evangelicals, unlike the Black Church, have been largely silent on the current issues of racism and systematic injustice (p. 11). McCaulley concludes the chapter with characteristics of Black Ecclesial Interpretation that include trusting, analyzing and grappling with the text of Scripture (p. 21).

In Chapter 2, McCaulley utilizes Romans 13:1-7 to derive a theology of policing but articulates that the passage involves more than "advocating for a passive populace that pays its taxes and defers to those in power," (p. 28). Romans 13:1-7 states that policing duties should never be a terror to those who are innocent (p. 28). The soldier is the closest equivalent to modern police (p. 42). McCaulley concludes that Paul's advice about submission to governing authorities must be read in the light of God's use of individuals to resist corrupt governments (p. 31). An example is John the Baptist as a critique to soldiers/police officers (p. 43). In Chapter 3, McCaulley notes that, for

Paul, this world is under the "domain of evil powers" who hold sway over the political, economic, and social policies of redeemed leaders and (pp. 59-60). In calling Rome Babylon, John likens her to the great oppressive empire that conquered Israel. Jesus, in the Sermon on the Mount, is presented as a divine king who provides for the Christian a way to witness in a world divided and torn by sin (p.84). The Black Church in its political witness hopes and works for a better world and in this pursuit finds an ally in the God of Israel (p. 70).

Chapter 4 demonstrates how the Bible is an aid in the pursuit of justice. McCaulley calls Luke "A Gospel Writer for Black Christians" and notes that Luke is the only writer in the New Testament who is probably Gentile (p. 74-75). The founding of the African Methodist Episcopal Church and the work of Richard Allen and Absalom Jones illustrates the plan of God in Luke for the reconciliation of all things encompassed by all people, including those of African descent (p.76). McCaulley connects the sonship of Jesus and the kingship of the Lord. The life of Jesus is compared to the nation of Israel. After the Baptism of Jesus, he is led by the Spirit into the wilderness to be tempted by Satan. This is reminiscent of the Exodus of the Children of Israel (p. 90). The conflation of Isaiah 61:1 and 58:6 in the ministry of Jesus is important. These passages as central pillars of Jesus' ministry speak directly to the hope and history of African-Americans. Chapter 5 examines the fundamental criticism of Black Christianity "as an alien thing, an imposition of the white man through the persuasive power of the whip and chain," (p. 75). Most of the early Christian centers were in the continents of Asia and Africa (p. 98). McCaulley demonstrates how the Old Testament tells the story of how the Hebrew people included and incorporated other ethnic groups into itself (p. 104). Turning to the New Testament, McCaulley notes the connection between the African presence at the beginning of Christianity and the Cross of Jesus (p.108). McCaulley also notes the vision of John in the book of Revelation that is universal and inclusive of all (p. 115).

Chapter 6 uses the psalms to address the issue of Black anger. McCaulley argues that Israel's pain and anger are recorded in the prophets, and the Psalter provides a means for processing grief. In the New Testament, the cross functions as the end of the cycle of vengeance and death. The Cross is a place where God enters our pain. The central themes of the resurrection, ascension, and final judgment are necessary in any account of Black anger and pain. The Incarnation is the presence of Christ, alongside the sufferer as a friend and a redeemer (p. 130). The Resurrection is God's affirmation of the value of people of African descent and a vindication of all Black hopes and dreams (p. 134). In Chapter 7, McCaulley examines what the Bible says about slavery. The Old and New Testament present the design of freedom for all people. The slave laws of the Torah provide limitation, regulation, and manumission (p. 145-146). The Torah provides for the dismantling of slavery. In the New Testament, in dealing with Paul's mention of slavery, these passages are often misunderstood and that Paul does not endorse slavery, but provides resources to dismantle it (p. 162).

*Reading While Black* is an excellent resource for understanding the nuances of African-American engagement with the Bible. McCaulley is rigorous in his analysis and articulates a "Black Ecclesial Interpretation" that is rooted in the Black Church experience. It is orthodox with a reverence for scripture, and engages social context and the history of systemic oppression. In each of the chapters, McCaulley begins with a personal anecdote or historical reference to an event in African-American history. With the same overall evangelical stance, the Black Church has addressed issues of injustice that have been and still are neglected by Euro-American evangelicals. The difference between Euro-American biblical interpretation and Black biblical interpretation highlights the importance of Black biblical interpretation. An example of this is the historical connection of the legacy of racism and modern-day policing. Slave patrols are the forerunner of modern American law enforcement. This connection helps one to understand the antagonism within policing that communities of color experience. This point of social location, which is a component of Black Ecclesial Interpretation, helps develop a system of policing that is fair and just for all members of society.

*Reading While Black* also emphasizes the clear and important role that both the continent of Africa and Africans have played in the development and the proliferation of the Gospel of Jesus Christ. Moreover, it is important to note that importance of Africa in both the Old and New Testaments. Additionally, there are some topics that are omitted in this excellent work. The issues of womanism, patriarchy within church leadership, and same-sex relationships are not discussed. However, McCaulley provides a framework for the continued dialogue of these issues. Esau McCaulley has provided a thoughtful, engaging, well-written and substantive book. It will challenge traditional Euro-centric biblical interpretation to be less parochial in perspective and broader in engagement. It provides a construct for Black ecclesial biblical interpretation that reflects both orthodoxy and contextual orthopraxy.

Cleotha Robertson<br>
Alliance Theological Seminary

*Say It!: Celebrating Expository Preaching in the African American Tradition*, Eric C. Redmond, Moody Publishers (ISBN: 978-0-8024-1920-0), 241 pp., $11.99 (paper)

*Say It!* is a discourse written unapologetically in celebration of African-American preaching's substance and style. More than a "how to book," the work offers anthropological import that speaks into the current climate of Black preaching. Editor Eric Redmond has compiled a group of contributors who testify to the way that the marriage of cultural relevance and expository preaching create a process and a proclamation that engages the mind and the soul of Black congregations. Redmond's purpose is to encourage and to edify, and this structure aligns with his experience as a pastor and professor. The encouragement comes in the form of a warning against impoverished preaching that removes the dynamism of contextualization and tenacious grounding in the biblical text. The edification occurs in the demonstrations of expository preaching provided by the contributors. Certainly, there is no shortage of books about African-American preaching culture, style, and methodology. This work itself references a multitude of offerings from homiletical giants such as Cleophus J. LaRue, Kenyatta Gilbert, and Frank Thomas. The how and what of Black preaching is a hot topic for those in and outside of the Christian and Black cultures. *Say It!* concisely names and establishes boldly the claim that "exposition and the tradition are best when they hang together," (p. 35). Moreover, it is a thorough contribution to the overall field of thoughtful and humble homiletical contemplation that seeks to magnify, glorify and proclaim the Gospel.

Charlie E. Dates provides a preface that sets the stage as he "seeks to provide a background for the biblical and colorful hermeneutic of black preaching," (p.13). In the midst of this journey, he suggests that

Black preachers shake off the "theological slave masters" (p.14) of white evangelicalism and European Enlightenment. This is a highly necessary and relevant point for the Black church overall, but it is particularly freeing for preachers who need to preach from a place of freedom in order to proclaim freedom. Dates shares that this is done by claiming ethnic affirmation and a sound exposition process. In the Introduction, Redmond provides a specific framework based on defining exposition and how it impacts "both the form and the content of preaching," (p. 24). Justice and hope are two of the main theological emphases manifested in Black preaching. This provides a direct connection to the why and what that often frames the needs of the Black congregation. These elements, along with the importance of celebration, create a strong, yet adaptable, base from which to view the significance of Black preaching. The next three parts of the work expand and demonstrate Redmond's hypothesis in more detail.

Part One gives a background of biblical exposition as it manifests within a Black hermeneutic. Winfred Omar Neely names human beings as storied creatures in need of locating their stories within the larger story of God (p.39). Redmond's contribution to Part One focuses on particular challenges with Old Testament exposition. These challenges surround the chronological vastness of the Old Testament, interpreting the various theological, moral and ethical dilemmas. The last chapter in Part One, presented by Ernest Gray, deals with the expositor negotiating the tension between cultural competence and the God-inspired practical application of the text's message. Part Two consists of examples of expository preaching from the Old Testament. George Parks, Jr., Redmond, Eric Mason, Terry D. Streeter, and Dates each invite the reader into their process of exposition for an Old Testament text. They also provide a manuscript of a sermon. This format is a definitive strength of the work, as it provides definitive examples. Admittedly, reading a manuscript is not the most enlivening way of revealing the dynamic marriage of cultural contextualization and exposition. The call and response is in fact another aspect of the world of the Black church, rather than merely a delivery technique. This is a limitation of the mode of communication, rather than a limitation of the creativity of the work itself.

The structure of Part Three falls in line with the structure developed in Part Two, as Romell Williams, Paul Felix, and K. Edward Copeland each present a New Testament exposition example and sermon manuscript. Williams handles the Gospels and Acts, Felix works with an epistle, and Copeland takes on the challenge of Revelation 21. Each of these contributors are concerned with the work of interpreting and building the bridge towards application for the preached word. In the Conclusion, Redmond advocates preaching every verse of Scripture as "the best way to make God's voice known to a congregation," (p. 218). The truth in this statement is easily taken for granted in the current church climate that can often lend itself to more of a "choose your own adventure" model of choosing preaching texts. Although this particular point is most immediately applicable for pastors who preach every, or at least most, Sundays, there is a path for occasional preachers as well. After Redmond provides points of advocacy and acknowledges points of possible objection, he aids those hoping to approach a preaching schedule in this way by offering a final section that is an instruction guide on how to preach through books. This guide is a compelling take away for further reflection.

One of the most engaging aspects of Parts Two and Three are the conclusions that each preacher includes after the sermon manuscripts. While each preacher takes a slightly different track in his approach, these conclusions are a bit of replay and commentary that is part confessional and part instructional. What were specific challenges to the exposition process and the contextual exegesis? There is a transparency offered, and this transparency represents a demonstration of humility and continuing curiosity about the process of preaching. The sermons are all different. This demonstrates that preachers can take a solid foundation of exposition and cultural investigation, and let it form in the message as God inspires in that individual preacher. This is not a formula. It is a methodology.

This reader would have loved to hear the contributions of some female preachers, for the purpose of expanding the viewpoint of the work to reflect the viewpoint of the Black church as a whole. Also, perhaps there could have also been a deeper exegesis of the intended audience. At times, I found myself asking, "Does the structure of the book exegete the audience for the book in a way that matches the proposed process of cultural exegesis and exposition for the Black church?" The root is there in the preface and introduction, but seems inconsistent in some of the following chapters. Redmond and his fellow contributors are successful in their goal to show the benefits for the Black church and Black preachers. This work stands out in that it names and challenges a growing trend of forsaking the foundations of the tradition. Many preachers are seeking to reconcile individual and group identity in and through God and the truth of the Gospel. This is a work that offers intellectual and spiritual aid in this endeavor. This work is one that does speak a needed truth into the arena of Black preaching and Black lived theology.

Jaclyn P. Williams<br>
Fuller Theological Seminary

www.ingramcontent.com/pod-product-compliance
Lightning Source LLC
Chambersburg PA
CBHW060356080526
44583CB00012B/336